KT-468-101

EAT. LIVE. GO.

FRESH FOOD FAST

EAT. LIVE. GO.
FRESH FOOD FAST

Donal Skehan

HODDER &
STOUGHTON

For my late grandmother, Elizabeth Ryan, who taught my family to cook and had an insatiable appetite for recipes from far and wide.

CONTENTS

It's said that life is all about the journey rather than the destination. Since I started writing recipes I have found that is most definitely the case, but perhaps there comes a point in everyone's life where you can sum up what you love best in the world in just three words. Eat, Live and Go are the three words that perfectly capture this space in time in my life and sum up what is most important to me. I wrote my last book *Fresh* as a means to take back control of life and the food I was eating and this book is a celebration of just that. Prioritising the food I eat, living a balanced lifestyle and taking time to travel and find inspiration from the world are all part of my current food story. This may all sound a little New Age, and maybe I have had just one too many green juices, but don't back away just yet.

This book is all about the journey, one that weaves through my love of food, trying to maintain balance in a busy world while at the same time enjoying some of the spectacular feasts and street eats I've experienced on my travels. I want this collection of recipes to inspire you and your family to enjoy those everyday moments, from small triumphs, panoramic views and epic sunsets to those grey days in between. To do that I want to arm you with an arsenal of recipes that take inspiration from cuisines across the world, from healthy dinners and quick food fixes to leisurely meals to enjoy around the table.

The book is split into three sections revolving around three core themes: food, lifestyle and travel. Eat is dedicated to the recipes which are quick and healthy, including hearty salads, lighter comfort foods and sweet indulgences. Live focuses on meals that pump you up and provide energy and nourishment, from restorative suppers, bright power breakfast ideas and superfood snacks. Finally, Go is dedicated to the food I've been inspired to create from my travels around the world over the last few years. The recurring theme throughout, you will notice, is an appetite for strong, bold flavours. All the recipes I've included, whether rich and indulgent or light and healthy, aim for full-on flavour. Nothing makes me more excited than trying new foods, experiencing new cultures and sharing them. Join me on the journey...

Dublin City Public Libraries

EAT

My mum always talks about the food my grandmother cooked in the seventies. It was surprisingly diverse, from curry to French pastries, much of it would have been unheard of in the home kitchens of the day. Her interest in foreign cuisines explored from an armchair was inspirational – she had a fearless confidence in good home cooking skills and the ability to turn her hand to some alien dish she had read about, in turn making it her own. Right up until she passed away we regularly spoke about the food I had tried on my travels and she was particularly fascinated by my visits to South East Asia. She left my family with a passion and an appetite for great food and for cooking in general. Among the many inspirations I have in the world of food, my grandmother's love of the simple pleasures of cooking continues to be the most grounding.

With ideas coming from all over the world as I travel, my repertoire is constantly expanding and it can often be difficult to define a set food style. Although my roots are in traditional Irish home cooking, I can't help but fall in love with dishes that are engrained with memories of certain times and far off places. The idea of food memories and dishes that instantly allow you to recall the moments when they were savoured is what is special to me. What it really comes back to, wherever I am in the world, is simple dishes that are full of flavour with little fuss, to be enjoyed with friends and family.

I never could have imagined when I first picked up a wooden spoon that food would play such a pivotal role in my life. I'm constantly inspired with each new ingredient I try or dish I enjoy. It can be mundane and routine or it can be fresh and exciting, but it is never the same twice. When it comes to everyday eating and the type of food I eat when I need quick solutions, it's the dishes that don't require a long list of ingredients, that can be made quickly and, most importantly, are worthwhile making that shine. More often than not I find myself going back to the same recipes, the ones that form a regular part of my repertoire of dishes. That's not to say that new dishes don't find their way into the mix, but there is satisfaction in knowing you have a small selection of recipes that are bulletproof.

With travel playing such a prominent role in my life over the past few years, it has meant my cooking style has changed somewhat. With a constantly changing kitchen setup, there recently came a need to declutter my collection of kitchen equipment. For a long time I have been guilty of hoarding a ridiculous amount of gadgets, including a Belgian waffle maker that comes out of hibernation about once a year. All these things were essential elements of my 'dream' kitchen, but having recently moved out of a kitchen of seven years, I've managed to whittle down this ominously heaving collection to but a few key items.

Whenever I read long lists of essential kitchen paraphernalia in cookbooks, I do wonder if most people reading them actually use any of it. Often they read as written by a crazed bride and groom, spewing out a fantasy wish list of kitchen gear that will never get used. For me it boils down to about ten key pieces. Obviously most recipes start with a sharp kitchen knife; food aficionados may disagree but any bog-standard knife will do as long as it's kept sharp. I use a medium-sized one that allows me to tackle most ingredients with ease, from the backbone of a chicken to an onion. Don't be tempted to buy a monstrous knife; it will more likely only damage your fingers and your ego. A reasonably sized wooden chopping board is all that's required and don't be lured in by novelty plastic ones. A good collection of mixing bowls in varying sizes is indispensible and can be used for anything, from making bread right down to collecting kitchen scraps as you work – mine are mainly metal and glass. You can agonise over the best frying pan, but when it comes down to frying an egg or whipping up an omelette, a good heavy-based non-stick frying pan with a metal handle for trips in and out of the oven wins every time. A sturdy casserole dish easily finds a prominent place on my list of key kitchenalia; spend money on a decent-sized one and it will be with you for life. For the lighter gear I would recommend a box grater, colander, peeler, hand-held mandoline and a salad spinner. The last one is essential – in a world filled with expensive pre-washed mixed salad bags, buying and washing your own salad leaves is well worth it. These few items and possibly a handful more are all you will need to make the recipes in this book. Of course, if you have the space and the inclination, go wild with egg timers, banana slicers, popcorn makers and electric corkscrews – please don't let me hold you back.

The recipes in this section are a good representation of the weekday and weekend cooking I do. I get great joy from dishes which are satisfyingly quick to prepare or that deliver a serious whack of heat, rounded spice or fresh tang. Meals like crispy Moroccan chicken salad humming with

North African spice or sticky Asian pork with braised greens sprinkled with toasted sesame seeds, prove that strong flavours can be delivered in a snap. This everyday eating swings from quick-fix meals to occasions when I am willing to take my time in the kitchen. Dishes that take longer to cook can often be prepared quickly and then left to take their time in the oven or on the stovetop. Chicken thighs braised in a creamy white wine sauce served with peppery salad leaves in a French mustard dressing or tender pieces of lamb stewed with dried fruits and store cupboard spices are perfect examples of this. This is the sort of cooking I prefer most when entertaining friends. It allows all the work to be done before the crowd descends and gives you time to enjoy yourself. Braised meats, crunchy salads, homemade breads, dipping sauces and grains tossed with roast vegetables are all part of my regular fare and make entertaining a pleasure.

These recipes are riffs on the cooking techniques I use regularly in my kitchen. Hearty, comforting, fresh and easily cooked in the home kitchen – when it comes down to it, there's not much more I want when I'm hungry.

QUICK
COOKING

One-Pan Singapore Noodles

Super Veg Roast Tomato Pasta

Fried Eggs with Brussels Sprouts and Pesto

Martha's One-Pan Pasta

Green Goddess Grilled Avocado Salad

Griddled Buttermilk Chicken Salad

Moroccan Crispy Chicken Salad

Beef and Beetroot Hummus Salad

Crispy Skin Salmon with Soba Noodles

Thai Chicken Burgers with Coriander Slaw

Smoky Flattened Chicken with Hummus, Seeds and Salad

Griddled Lamb Steaks with Bean Stew

Sticky Asian Pork with Sesame Greens

Whenever I get asked what recipes you should try first from a new cookbook, I always say go for the quick-cook ones - and of course the desserts! There's far less commitment time-wise and the ingredients lists tend to be shorter. In order to get yourself quick-cooking ready, shopping for core standby ingredients is essential. Money is well spent on staples like grains, pulses, pasta and tins of good things – these will help make up your speedy supper armoury.

At the core of these recipes, however, is a dedication to delivering serious flavour in a short amount of time. For that I rely on spices, fresh herbs, store cupboard ingredients like noodles, pasta, tins of tomatoes and beans, and fresh vegetables. Take the recipe for One-pan Singapore Noodles: in theory, a glorified pot noodle; in practice, a clever method using fresh veggies and quick-cook rice noodles combined with pantry sauces and spices to make a meal in under 15 minutes. Instant satisfaction.

For a heartier supper in minutes, lamb steaks flash-fried in a hot pan until just blushing and charred and served with a cannellini bean stew, sweet with cherry tomatoes are a real winner, while Smoky Flattened Chicken with Hummus, Seeds and Salad is a great example of a fresh and flavourful speedy supper that doesn't disappoint.

After a recent stay in a house with a limited kitchen, my love for one-pan dishes has grown. These Singapore noodles lend themselves well to the one-pan cause as they use rice vermicelli noodles. The noodles come alive with only a brief lick of boiling liquid and wrapped up with curry powder, tender vegetables and Asian ingredients, consider your supper served!

Hands-on time: 15 minutes | Total time: 15 minutes

ONE-PAN SINGAPORE NOODLES

SERVES 4

1 tbsp sunflower oil

3 garlic cloves, finely minced

1 large thumb-sized piece of fresh ginger, finely chopped

2 red chillies, thinly sliced

6 spring onions, thinly sliced

100g green beans, trimmed

1 red pepper, deseeded and thinly sliced

1 tbsp curry powder

100g frozen peas

3 tbsp dark soy sauce

1 tbsp rice wine

1 tsp sugar

1 tsp sesame oil

225g rice vermicelli

300ml boiling hot chicken stock

Large handful of fresh coriander, roughly chopped

1 Heat the oil in a large wok over a high heat and stir-fry the garlic, ginger, chilli and spring onions for 2 minutes until the onions are just tender.

2 Add the green beans and red pepper and stir-fry for a further 4 minutes before stirring in the curry powder, frozen peas, soy sauce, rice wine, sugar and sesame oil.

3 Roughly break in the noodles and pour over the chicken stock, making sure the noodles are completely submerged. Continue to stir until the noodles are tender; which should only take a couple of minutes, by which time the liquid should also have evaporated.

4 Serve in deep bowls with a generous sprinkle of coriander.

This pasta dish is one I come back to time and time again. I've been making versions of it since I first left home and the one main reason is because of its simplicity. You simply roast Mediterranean vegetables until caramelised, add warm pasta to the roasting tin, toss to get everything acquainted and serve straight to the table!

Hands-on time: 15 minutes | Total time: 45 minutes

SUPER VEG ROAST TOMATO PASTA

SERVES 2

200g cherry tomatoes, sliced in half

1 small aubergine, cut into 2cm cubes

2 courgettes, cut into 2cm cubes

2 red onions, quartered but roots left intact

1 head of garlic, top sliced off

4 tbsp olive oil

2 tbsp balsamic vinegar

1 tsp chilli flakes

200g penne

Sea salt

Parmesan shavings, to serve

Large handful of basil leaves, to serve

1 Preheat the oven to 200°C (180°C fan).

2 Arrange the tomatoes, aubergine, courgette, red onions and garlic in separate piles across a medium-sized roasting tin with high sides. Drizzle over the olive oil and balsamic vinegar and sprinkle with sea salt and chilli flakes. Give everything a good shuffle to make sure it's all coated evenly, then place in the oven to roast on the middle shelf for 30 minutes.

3 About 10 minutes before the vegetables are finished cooking, cook the pasta in a large pan of boiling salted water until al dente.

4 Remove the roasting tin from the oven and carefully squeeze the mushy garlic out of the skins on to the tomatoes; discard the skins. Using the back of a fork, mash down the garlic and tomatoes until combined. Add a ladle of the pasta cooking liquid to this and stir to make a sauce. Now mix all of the contents of the pan together and then pour in the drained pasta.

5 Add some generous shavings of Parmesan and roughly tear in a few basil leaves. Toss everything together until well combined and serve hot, garnished with more Parmesan shavings and basil leaves.

This is a simple dish that can easily be made with regular shop-bought pesto but comes alive with the homemade version below. It makes quite a lot of pesto but I'm of the opinion that if you're going to go to the trouble, you may as well make enough to use another time, whether stirred into pasta or simply spread on toast. If you have time you could roast the Brussels sprouts instead of frying, which will only add to the taste and texture – place in a small roasting pan with a drizzle of olive oil and roast for 30 minutes at 200°C (180°C fan).

Hands-on time: 25 minutes | **Total time: 25 minutes**

FRIED EGGS WITH BRUSSELS SPROUTS AND PESTO

SERVES 2

1–2 tbsp olive oil

500g Brussels sprouts, trimmed and sliced in half

4 large free-range eggs

Grated Parmesan, to serve

FOR THE PESTO

200g basil (leaves and stalks)

100g pine nuts

75g Parmesan, grated

250ml extra-virgin olive oil

2 garlic cloves, minced

Juice of ½ lemon

Sea salt and freshly ground black pepper

1 First make the pesto. Blitz all the ingredients in a food processor until the mixture becomes smooth. Taste and adjust the seasoning and add a little extra olive oil if you feel the pesto is too thick.

2 Place a frying pan over a medium-high heat and add a drop of olive oil. When it's hot, add the sprouts and pan fry for 6–8 minutes, stirring occasionally and allowing them to catch every so slightly. At the end of the cooking time, add a few tablespoons of water and cover with a lid. Cook for a further few minutes or until the sprouts are just tender. Transfer to a mixing bowl.

3 Add a tablespoon of oil to the same pan and fry the eggs until the white is no longer translucent but the yolk is still loose and runny.

4 While the eggs are still cooking toss the sprouts with a few tablespoons of pesto and transfer to two serving plates (transfer any unused pesto to a jar with a tight-fitting lid, top up with a layer of extra-virgin olive oil and store in the fridge for up to 5 days). Top with the fried eggs and sprinkle with a little grated Parmesan and a sprinkle of black pepper. Serve straight away.

A brilliantly sim... ...American food writer and domestic godde... ...art, which sees both pasta and sauce all cooked in the ... pan, resulting in perfectly al dente spaghetti wrapped in a silky spinach and tomato sauce.

Hands-on time: 10 minutes | Total time: 15 minutes

MARTHA'S ONE-PAN PASTA

SERVES 2

200g cherry tomatoes, sliced in half

100g baby spinach leaves

1 small onion, thinly sliced

3 garlic cloves, thinly sliced

1 red chilli, finely chopped

200g spaghetti

2 tbsp extra-virgin olive oil

600ml chicken stock or water

50g pecorino cheese, grated

Small handful of basil leaves, roughly chopped

Sea salt and freshly ground black pepper

1 Arrange the tomatoes, spinach, onion, garlic, and chilli across the base of a wide, deep frying pan. Nestle the spaghetti in the centre of the pan and pour over the olive oil and chicken stock or water.

2 Place the pan over a medium-high heat and bring the contents of the pan to the boil. Cook for about 9 minutes, stirring the pasta regularly with a pair of kitchen tongs until it's cooked and the liquid has nearly evaporated to create a sauce.

3 Remove the pan from the heat and stir though the pecorino cheese and basil. Season with salt and pepper to serve.

Essentially a deconstructed guacamole, this salad takes the key elements of the classic Mexican dip and puts them front and centre. Grilling the avocados provides a smoky note but it is essential you use firm, ripe avocados that won't leave you with a mushy hot mess. The dressing is smooth, creamy and vibrantly green, perfect for those days when only virtuous will do!

Hands-on time: 10 minutes | Total time: 10 minutes

GREEN GODDESS GRILLED AVOCADO SALAD

SERVES 4

2½ large firm and ripe avocados

Rapeseed oil, for brushing

3 baby gem lettuces, leaves separated

200g cherry tomatoes, sliced in half

Large handful of coriander leaves

1 red onion, thinly sliced

Sea salt and freshly ground black pepper

FOR THE DRESSING

½ ripe avocado

Small handful of fresh chives

1 tbsp white wine vinegar

2–3 tbsp extra-virgin olive oil

1 garlic clove

Juice of ½ lime

1 tsp hot sauce

1 tsp honey

1 Cut the avocados in half, remove the stones and scoop out the flesh so the halves remain intact.

2 Place one avocado half along with all the other ingredients for the dressing in a food processor and blitz until smooth. You should be left with a runny dressing but if you find it becomes too thick, loosen with a few more tablespoons of extra-virgin olive oil.

3 Place a griddle pan over a medium-high heat. Brush the remaining avocados with a little oil and then place in the pan to griddle for 2–3 minutes on each side, or until they have deep char marks. Remove from the pan, allow to cool and then split the avocado halves into quarters.

4 Arrange the remaining salad ingredients on a serving platter and top with the grilled avocado quarters. Season with salt and pepper, then drizzle over the salad dressing and serve.

A simple salad like this one is underrated. Marinating the chicken with buttermilk, thyme and lemon zest will result in tender meat that is pretty irresistible when charred on a griddle pan; the perfect combination with a creamy, sharp dressing such as this one.

Hands-on time: 30 minutes | Total time: 30 minutes, plus marinating

GRIDDLED BUTTERMILK CHICKEN SALAD

SERVES 2

100ml buttermilk

Few thyme sprigs, leaves picked

Zest and juice of ½ lemon

2 chicken breasts (about 150g each)

½ romaine lettuce, leaves torn

100g rocket leaves

Grated Parmesan

1 tbsp rapeseed oil

2 slices of sourdough bread

1 large ripe avocado, thinly sliced

Sea salt and freshly ground black pepper

FOR THE DRESSING

100ml natural yoghurt

1 tsp Dijon mustard

2 tbsp extra-virgin olive oil

2 tsp Worcestershire sauce

Zest and juice of ½ lemon

2 anchovy fillets

1 In a small mixing bowl, whisk together the buttermilk, thyme leaves, lemon zest and juice and season with salt and pepper. Add the chicken breasts and toss to coat completely. Put to one side to marinate for 15 minutes, or covered in the fridge for up to 24 hours.

2 Put the ingredients for the dressing into a small food processor and blitz until smooth. Pour the dressing into a large mixing bowl, add the lettuce and rocket and sprinkle over a grating of Parmesan. Toss to coat just before the chicken is cooked.

3 Place a griddle pan over a medium-high heat and brush with a little oil. Cook the sourdough slices for 2–3 minutes on each side and set aside; reduce the heat. Remove the chicken from the bowl, shaking off any excess marinade, and place on the griddle pan to cook for 8 minutes on each side. Meanwhile cut the griddled bread into rough cubes.

4 When the chicken is cooked remove from the pan and slice thinly. Serve the tossed salad leaves in deep bowls topped with the chicken, sourdough croutons and slices of avocado.

Chicken thighs are one of my favourite parts of the chicken – both to cook and to eat. Cooked slowly skin-side down in a fuzzy dust of North African spices, they are simply irresistible. Savour them warm from the pan or with this fresh and hearty salad, which is easily adapted with whatever appropriate ingredients your fridge may offer.

Hands-on time: 20 minutes | Total time: 30 minutes

MOROCCAN CRISPY CHICKEN SALAD

SERVES 4

1 tbsp rapeseed oil

1 tsp ground turmeric

1 tbsp smoked paprika

1 tsp cayenne pepper

1 tsp ground cumin

1 tsp ground coriander

4–6 boneless chicken thighs, skin on

Sea salt and freshly ground black pepper

FOR THE SALAD

200g cooked bulgur wheat

1 x 400g tin chickpeas, rinsed and drained

1 large cucumber, seeds removed and chopped in cubes

1 small red onion, thinly sliced

2 tomatoes, roughly diced

1 x 250g jar roasted red peppers, drained and roughly diced

Large handful of flat-leaf parsley, roughly chopped

FOR THE DRESSING

6 tbsp extra-virgin olive oil

Juice of 1 lemon

1 tbsp red wine vinegar

1 garlic clove, finely minced

Sea salt and freshly ground black pepper

1 In a bowl whisk together the oil and all the spices and then add the chicken thighs, massaging them with the spicy oil. Season with salt and pepper.

2 Place a large frying pan over a low-medium heat and fry the chicken, skin-side down, for 8–10 minutes, by which time the skin should be super crispy. Turn and cook for a further 8 minutes on the other side, or until cooked through.

3 While the chicken is cooking whisk together the ingredients for the dressing and season to taste.

4 Place all the ingredients for the salad in a mixing bowl and pour over the dressing. Toss to mix through and coat and then serve up with the spiced chicken thighs, still hot from the pan.

Use the best dry-aged steaks you can afford and make sure you give them plenty of time to rest before serving to allow all the juices to settle. Za'atar seasoning can be found in most supermarkets but if you can't find it, use a pestle and mortar to pound together 2 tablespoons sesame seeds, 4 teaspoons cumin seeds, 4 teaspoons ground sumac, 1 teaspoon sea salt and 1 tablespoon dried oregano. This mixture will keep for up to 6 months in an airtight jar and is delicious sprinkled over flatbreads or as a coating for pan-fried chicken.

Hands-on time: 25 minutes | Total time: 25–30 minutes, plus marinating and resting

BEEF AND BEETROOT HUMMUS SALAD

SERVES 2–4

2 sirloin steaks (225g each), about 4cm thick

4 tbsp za'atar

1 tbsp rapeseed oil

FOR THE BEETROOT HUMMUS

2 cooked beetroot

½ x 400g tin chickpeas, rinsed and drained

1 small garlic clove, roughly chopped

1 tsp ground cumin

1 tbsp pomegranate molasses, plus extra to drizzle

1½ tsp tahini

Juice of ½ lemon

Sea salt and freshly ground black pepper

FOR THE PICKLED CUCUMBER SALAD

2 baby cucumbers or ½ regular cucumber

4 tbsp rice wine vinegar

2 tbsp caster sugar

½ small red onion, very thinly sliced

6 fresh mint leaves

1 tbsp toasted sesame seeds

1 Pat the steaks dry with kitchen paper and use your hands to press the za'atar on to both sides of the steaks. If you have time, cover with foil or cling film and leave at room temperature for 2–3 hours to allow the flavours to permeate.

2 For the beetroot hummus, blitz all the ingredients together in a food processor until smooth. Season to taste.

3 To make the cucumber salad, place each cucumber on a chopping board and use a swivel vegetable peeler to pare into long thin ribbons.

Place the vinegar in a large bowl and stir in the sugar to dissolve. Add the cucumber ribbons with the sliced red onion and toss to coat. Cover with cling film and leave for at least 10 minutes, or up to 8 hours in the fridge.

4 Heat the rapeseed oil in a large, heavy-based frying pan over a high heat. Add the steaks and cook for 3–4 minutes on each side. Transfer the steaks to a plate, season with salt and set aside in a warm place to rest, covered in foil, for about 5 minutes before carving into thin slices.

5 To serve, drain off any excess liquid from the cucumber salad, then tear the mint leaves into small pieces and fold into the salad with the toasted sesame seeds. Arrange on plates with the sliced beef. Add a large dollop of the beetroot hummus, drizzled with a little extra pomegranate molasses.

Salmon skin cooked until sizzling, crisp and golden is such a treat and it could not be easier to achieve. By frying the salmon skin-side down and – more importantly – resisting the temptation to flip it over before it's time, you will be left with tender flesh and that all-important crisp skin. With a lick of salty soy sauce and the clean acidity of rice wine, you are left with a rather simple Asian-inspired supper.

Hands-on time: 30 minutes | Total time: 30–35 minutes, plus marinating and resting

CRISPY SKIN SALMON
WITH SOBA NOODLES

SERVES 4

1 tbsp soy sauce

1 tbsp rice wine

1 thumb-sized piece of fresh ginger, finely grated

1 garlic clove, finely minced

1 tsp sesame oil

4 salmon fillets (about 100g each)

1 tbsp sunflower oil

1 tbsp sesame seeds, toasted

FOR THE NOODLES

250g buckwheat soba noodles

1 tbsp sunflower oil

6 spring onions, thinly sliced

1 garlic clove, thinly sliced

200g sugar snap peas

1 tbsp soy sauce

1 tsp sesame oil

1 In a wide dish whisk together the soy sauce, rice wine, ginger, garlic and sesame oil. Add the salmon fillets and toss gently until completely coated. Leave to marinate for 10 minutes or up to 2 hours.

2 Meanwhile prepare the noodles. Soak the noodles in boiling water for 3 minutes until tender. Drain and rinse under cold water and set aside.

3 Heat a wok over a high heat, add the oil and then fry the spring onions and garlic for 2 minutes. Add the sugar snap peas and stir-fry for 3–4 minutes. Add the drained noodles to the wok and pour in the soy sauce and sesame oil. Stir-fry for a further 2–3 minutes until the noodles are heated through and no liquid remains. Keep warm while you cook the salmon.

4 To cook the salmon heat a frying pan over a medium-high heat and add the sunflower oil. Fry the salmon fillets for 5–6 minutes, skin-side down, until the flesh is almost all completely opaque and the skin is sizzling and crisp. Flip and fry until just cooked through, about 2–3 minutes.

5 Serve the salmon on top of generous mounds of the noodles. Add a sprinkle of sesame seeds and get stuck in!

An instant hit of Asian street food with enough vegetable action to make you feel you're treating yourself well. I'm slightly uneasy about adding mayonnaise to the coleslaw, for fear of upsetting the authenticity police, but with only a small amount it adds a much-needed creaminess to this crunchy and aromatic salad. Use chicken or turkey mince here to cut out the need for a food processor.

Hands-on time: 30 minutes | **Total time: 30 minutes**

THAI CHICKEN BURGERS
WITH CORIANDER SLAW

SERVES 4

3 garlic cloves, roughly chopped

Large handful coriander

1 red chilli, roughly chopped

Zest and juice of ½ lime

500g chicken breasts, roughly chopped (or use minced chicken)

1 tbsp fish sauce

6 spring onions, thinly sliced

1–2 tbsp rapeseed oil

FOR THE CORIANDER SLAW

4 tbsp mayonnaise

2 tsp sriracha sauce, plus extra to serve

Juice of ½ lime

½ small head of red cabbage, finely shredded

2 carrots, grated

Large handful of coriander, roughly chopped

4 tbsp salted peanuts, toasted

1 Place the garlic, coriander, red chilli and lime zest in a food processor and blitz until smooth. Add the chicken, lime juice, fish sauce and half the spring onions and blitz until you are left with a smooth paste.

2 Transfer to a bowl and stir through the remaining spring onions. Form the mixture into eight small burger-sized patties and leave to rest on a plate.

3 For the coriander slaw, mix together all the ingredients until evenly coated. Cover and place in the fridge until ready to serve.

4 Heat a frying pan over a medium-high heat and add the oil. Fry the chicken burgers for 3–4 minutes on each side until golden brown and cooked all the way through.

5 Serve the burgers with a generous side of coriander slaw and a splat of sriracha sauce to dip into.

This supper is inspired by a recipe from Diana Henry, whose wonderful cookbook and ode to the chicken, *A Bird in the Hand*, is filled with recipes dedicated to all things fowl. While the herby paste in Diana's recipe is used for a spatchcocked chicken (equally delicious by the way), I've used it here for a speedier supper with chicken breasts.

Hands-on time: 25–30 minutes | Total time: 25–30 minutes, plus marinating

SMOKY FLATTENED CHICKEN WITH HUMMUS, SEEDS AND SALAD

SERVES 4

4 chicken breasts (about 150g each)

150g rocket leaves

1–2 tbsp extra-virgin olive oil

3 tbsp pumpkin seeds, toasted

FOR THE MARINADE

4 tbsp olive oil

Juice of ½ lemon

3 garlic cloves

1 small red chilli

Large handful of coriander

Large handful of flat-leaf parsley

FOR THE HUMMUS

1 x 400g tin chickpeas, rinsed and drained

1 tbsp tahini

1 garlic clove, finely minced

½ tsp smoked paprika

½ tsp ground cumin

½ tsp cayenne pepper

Juice of ½ lemon

Sea salt

1 Put all the ingredients for the marinade in a food processor and process until blitzed, scraping down the sides as you go. Transfer to a wide, shallow dish and clean the food processor.

2 Butterfly the chicken: place a chicken breast on a chopping board and, with your hand flat on the top of it, use a sharp knife to slice into the thickest part of the breast. Do not slice all the way through. Open out the chicken so it resembles a butterfly and repeat with the other chicken breasts. Place in the dish with the marinade and turn to coat, massaging the marinade into the chicken. Leave to sit for at least 15 minutes or up to 6 hours if you have the time.

3 For the hummus, blitz all the ingredients until smooth, keeping a little of the lemon juice aside. Season with salt to taste. If your mixture looks too thick, simply loosen it with a little water.

4 Heat a griddle pan over a high heat, add the chicken breasts and cook for 3–4 minutes on each side or until cooked all the way through. Press down heavily on the chicken as it cooks using a metal spatula.

5 In a bowl, drizzle the rocket with a little extra-virgin olive oil and pour over the remaining lemon juice. Add the seeds and toss through.

6 To serve, spread a generous dollop of hummus across the plate, top with the chicken and place a handful of the rocket salad on top.

Lamb has always held a sense of celebration for me, something to be enjoyed on a special occasion, when a roast would be presented to the dinner table with gusto. For the occasional dinner in my house growing up, my mom would grill lamb chops until the fat went crispy and sweet and then sprinkle with sea salt – a total treat. These grilled lamb steaks are easy to prepare and can be served with just a simply dressed salad for a light meal. But served with a bean stew enriched with cherry tomatoes and spinach, dinner is only moments away.

Hands-on time: 25 minutes | Total time: 25–30 minutes

GRIDDLED LAMB STEAKS
WITH BEAN STEW

SERVES 2

2 lamb steaks (about 200g each)

2 tbsp olive oil

1 tbsp balsamic vinegar

2 garlic cloves, finely minced

1 rosemary sprig, leaves finely chopped

1 onion, finely chopped

250g cherry tomatoes, sliced in half

250ml chicken stock

1 x 400g tin cannellini beans, rinsed and drained

250g baby spinach leaves

Sea salt and freshly ground black pepper

1 Massage the lamb steaks with 1 tablespoon of the olive oil, the balsamic vinegar, 1 garlic clove, the rosemary and a generous amount of salt and pepper. Set aside.

2 In a frying pan over a medium-high heat, fry the onion in the remaining olive oil for 6–8 minutes until tender. Add the remaining garlic and cherry tomatoes. Fry for a further 3–4 minutes. Add the chicken stock and beans and bring to a steady simmer.

3 Add the spinach to the pan and slowly stir through to wilt down. Remove from the heat and season to taste.

4 Fry the lamb steaks on a griddle pan over a high heat for 2–3 minutes on each side, depending on the thickness of your steak. Allow the lamb to rest on a warm plate, covered, for a few minutes before serving with the bean stew.

A simple Asian-inspired one-pan supper, which can be adapted with beef, chicken or prawns. I get great satisfaction out of dishes that can be served to the table in the pan or pot they were cooked in – perhaps it's the over the top lid removal to reveal steaming deliciousness and the 'oohs' and 'aahs' that follow from your guests – anyone else? I guess I'm just a sucker for the drama of the reveal! Regardless of how you do choose to serve, with or without flourish, here you can enjoy the gratification of creating sticky pork and tender vegetables in a matter of minutes.

Hands-on time: 30 minutes | **Total time: 35 minutes**

STICKY ASIAN PORK
WITH SESAME GREENS

SERVES 4

500g whole pork fillet, trimmed

1 tbsp Chinese five-spice powder

1 tbsp sunflower oil

1 large thumb-sized piece of fresh ginger, finely minced

3 garlic cloves, finely minced

1 red chilli, finely chopped

3 tbsp rice wine

3 tbsp oyster sauce

1 tbsp dark brown sugar

2 large bok choy, cut into quarters

200g sugar snap peas

1 tbsp sesame seeds, toasted

1 Slice the fillet in half and roll both halves in the five-spice powder until completely coated.

2 Place a large frying pan over a medium heat and add the oil. Fry the pork fillet for 16–18 minutes or until it has a good colour on all sides (if you have a meat thermometer the internal temperature should be 65°C). Remove the pork and place on a plate to rest.

3 Using the oil left in the pan fry the ginger, garlic and the chilli for 2 minutes. Add in the rice wine, oyster sauce, sugar and 150ml boiling water. Simmer gently for 3–4 minutes until slightly reduced.

4 Return the pork to the pan, place the bok choy and sugar snap peas around it and cover with a lid. Cook over a medium heat for 4 minutes until the vegetables are tender.

5 Before serving, remove the pork from the pan, slice it into medallions and it nudge back into the centre of the pan, spooning over the sauce to coat. Serve the whole pan straight to the table with a sprinkle of toasted sesame seeds.

TIME
TO COOK

———

Sweet Potato Nachos

———

Roast Cauliflower and Chickpea Platter

———

Chilli Lemongrass Rice and Eggs

———

Autumn Grain Salad

———

Sweet Potato Gnocchi with Kale and Sage Butter

———

Chicken Katsu Curry

———

Spice Rub Chicken Leg Supper

———

White Wine Chicken Thighs with French Mustard Salad

———

Arroz Con Pollo

———

Grilled Indian Yoghurt Chicken with Spiced Vegetables

———

Sticky Fish Sauce Chicken

———

Moroccan Lamb Stew

———

Shepherd's Pie with Cauliflower Champ Mash

———

As much as I love dinners that are quick to cook, I think I get most enjoyment in the kitchen from slow-cook suppers that just bubble or simmer away, allowing you the opportunity to experiment, to taste, to improve and to savour the often-overlooked pleasure of cooking. Maybe it's the old romantic in me, but lately I've taken to cooking with jazz music playing in the background; it's soothing and makes the whole experience quite relaxing. It sets the perfect tone for stews blipping away on the stove top, filling the kitchen with tempting aromas and good vibes. Now I promise I'm not going to start lighting candles in an attempt to seduce you into trying these recipes – hopefully they will be tempting enough in themselves.

It's this idea of relaxed time spent in the kitchen that conjures up the type of dishes this chapter is all about: rich shepherd's pie with a creamy cauliflower mash, crispy chicken legs generously massaged with oil and a colourful spice rub served up with tender roast carrots and red onion, or chicken thighs slowly braised in white wine and thyme, served with glossy green leaves. Humble and filling grub that is worth waiting for.

Nacho purists please look away now, because while this recipe may tick a few boxes, it is certainly not true to the original; I've used chunky roast sweet potato chips instead of tortilla chips as a base for a slightly healthier variation. It's satisfying and filling and guaranteed to win at least a few fans! Instead of serving the roasted sweet potatoes in one big tray, you could divide into smaller roasting tins and serve as individual portions.

Hands-on time: 15 minutes | Total time: 35–40 minutes

SWEET POTATO NACHOS

SERVES 4

2 medium sweet potatoes, cut into chunky chips

2 red onions, sliced into eighths

1 tbsp sunflower oil

2 tsp paprika

1 tsp cayenne pepper

1 x 200g jar jalapeño peppers, drained

1 x 400g tin black beans, rinsed and drained

200g Cheddar cheese, grated

6 spring onions, thinly sliced

75g soured cream

Salsa, to serve (see page 161)

Sea salt

FOR THE GUACAMOLE

1 ripe avocado, halved and stone removed

Juice of ½ lime

Large handful of coriander, plus extra to garnish

½ tsp Tabasco sauce

Sea salt

1 Preheat the oven to 220°C (200°C fan).

2 Place the sweet potatoes and red onions on a large baking tray (use two baking trays if necessary – it's important that the vegetables have space to cook otherwise they will steam and go soggy). Drizzle with sunflower oil and toss with the paprika, cayenne and sea salt until completely coated. Roast in the oven for 25–30 minutes or until the sweet potato is tender and slightly charred at the edges.

3 For the guacamole, blitz all the ingredients together in a food processor until smooth. Season to taste with sea salt.

4 When the sweet potatoes are cooked, pile them up on one baking tray and top with the jalapenos, black beans, Cheddar and half the spring onions. Return to the oven for a further 5–6 minutes or until the cheese is melted and golden.

5 Serve with a generous scattering of the remaining spring onions, coriander, and dollops of soured cream, guacamole and the salsa.

There is exotic pleasure in this clatter of Middle Eastern flavours and ingredients, with hunks of tender charred cauliflower at the steering wheel. Bulk this great vegetable platter out with some cooked grains, such as bulgur wheat or pearl barley.

Hands-on time: 15 minutes | **Total time: 45 minutes**

ROAST CAULIFLOWER
AND CHICKPEA PLATTER

SERVES 4

2 heads of cauliflower, cut into quarters

1 x 400g tin chickpeas, rinsed and drained

3 tbsp rapeseed oil

1 tbsp sumac

1 tbsp ground cumin

1 tbsp ground coriander

1 tsp cayenne pepper

1 pomegranate

2 tbsp pomegranate molasses

25g pine nuts, toasted

Large handful of fresh coriander, roughly chopped

FOR THE TAHINI DRESSING

4 tbsp tahini

Juice of ½ lemon

1 garlic clove, very finely chopped

1 tsp sumac

1 tsp ground cumin

1 tsp ground coriander

1 Preheat the oven to 200°C (180°C fan).

2 Place the cauliflower and chickpeas into a large roasting dish and drizzle with the oil. Sprinkle with the spices and toss until the chickpeas and cauliflower pieces are completely coated. Roast in the oven for 35 minutes until the cauliflower is charred and the chickpeas are crispy.

3 Whisk together the ingredients for the dressing until combined. Loosen with 5 tablespoons of water and set aside.

4 Cut the pomegranate in half and, holding one half cut side down over a bowl, bash with a wooden spoon to release the seeds. Repeat with the other half.

5 Arrange the cooked cauliflower and chickpeas on a serving platter and drizzle with the tahini dressing and pomegranate molasses. Sprinkle over the pomegranate seeds, pine nuts and coriander and serve.

Anyone who has travelled in South East Asia will no doubt have experienced the diverse food and culture that exists there. There are plenty of dishes that borrow ingredients from neighbouring countries and cultures. One such dish is a chilli and lemongrass chicken recipe that I picked up along the way in Vietnam; the ingredients are a perfect example of this diversity, combining salty Thai fish sauce with earthy spice from Indian curry powder to create a sweet and spicy sauce. I have taken some serious liberties and borrowed the core ingredients to create a riff on an Anglo-Indian classic – a sort of South East Asian kedgeree.

Hands-on time: 15 minutes | Total time: 30 minutes

CHILLI LEMONGRASS RICE AND EGGS

SERVES 4

1 tbsp sunflower oil

3 lemongrass stalks, very thinly sliced

3 garlic cloves, thinly sliced

2 red chillies, thinly sliced

6 spring onions, thinly sliced

1 heaped tbsp medium curry powder

300g basmati rice, washed and drained

750ml chicken stock

20 fresh raw tiger prawns, peeled and deveined

Large handful of basil and coriander leaves, roughly chopped

1 tbsp fish sauce

4 soft-boiled eggs, peeled and halved

1 Heat a large, high-sided pan over a medium-high heat and add the oil. Add the lemongrass, garlic and half the chilli and spring onions and fry for 2 minutes, before stirring through the curry powder.

2 Add the rice and stir through the spice mixture until combined. Pour over the chicken stock and bring to a steady simmer. Cover with a lid and cook for 15 minutes or until the liquid has been completely absorbed.

3 Five minutes before the rice is done and while there is still some liquid in the pan, lay the prawns across the top of the rice and cover with a lid. Cook until the prawns are firm and no longer translucent.

4 Fluff up the rice with a fork and mix through half the herbs and the fish sauce. Arrange the warm, soft-boiled egg halves on top of the rice and sprinkle with the remaining herbs, chilli and spring onions to serve.

Grains like pearl barley, faro and bulgur wheat all have a long list of health benefits but are also fairly inexpensive and fantastic store cupboard fillers. You can use any of the above grains in this salad – mixed with a combination of sweet and tender roasted squash, charred, slightly bitter radicchio and smoky red peppers, it comes alive.

Hands-on time: 15 minutes | Total time: 60 minutes

AUTUMN GRAIN SALAD

SERVES 4

1 large butternut squash, peeled, deseeded and cut into 3cm thick slices

2–3 tbsp rapeseed oil

1 tbsp honey

1 tsp red chilli flakes

2 heads of radicchio, cored and quartered

250g pearl barley, cooked

100g rocket leaves

90g roasted red peppers from a jar, sliced

4 tbsp toasted seeds (sesame, pumpkin, sunflower etc)

Sea salt and freshly ground black pepper

FOR THE DRESSING

3 tbsp extra-virgin olive oil

1 tbsp white wine vinegar

1 tsp honey

1 tsp Dijon mustard

1 garlic clove, very finely chopped

Sea salt and freshly ground black pepper

1 Preheat the oven to 200°C (180°C fan).

2 Place the squash slices in a roasting tray and drizzle with 2 tablespoons of the oil and the honey. Sprinkle over the chilli flakes and season with salt and pepper and toss to coat. Roast in the oven for 45 minutes or until tender and slightly charred and caramelised on the outside.

3 While the squash is roasting prepare the dressing by shaking together all the ingredients in a jar with a tight-fitting lid.

4 When the squash is nearly ready, heat a griddle pan or frying pan over a high heat. Rub the radicchio quarters with the remaining oil and season with salt and pepper. Char the radicchio on all sides and then transfer to a plate.

5 Place the cooked pearl barley, rocket leaves and red pepper slices in a bowl. Add most of the dressing, reserving a little to drizzle over the top at the end, and toss through.

6 To serve, divide the dressed grains between four plates and top with the charred radicchio, roasted squash and toasted seeds. Finish with an extra drizzle of the dressing (or some extra-virgin olive oil).

The idea of homemade pasta can be fairly off-putting if you've never made it before. I see gnocchi as pasta's less sophisticated cousin that is far easier to prepare at home. While they may be clumpy these sweet potato gnocchi dumplings, creamy with ricotta, are as classy as they come. Served with kale in a nutty butter and sage sauce, they are perfection, even if I do say so myself.

Hands-on time: 20 minutes | **Total time: 1 hour, plus resting**

SWEET POTATO GNOCCHI
WITH KALE AND SAGE BUTTER

SERVES 4

2 large sweet potatoes

100g ricotta cheese

50g Parmesan, finely grated, plus extra to serve

Grating of fresh nutmeg

½ tsp freshly ground black pepper

1 tsp fresh thyme leaves, finely chopped

1 large free-range egg

150g plain flour, plus extra for dusting

FOR THE KALE AND SAGE BUTTER

100g butter

3 tbsp olive oil

4 garlic cloves, finely chopped

3 sage sprigs, leaves removed and thinly sliced

200g kale, leaves torn from stem and roughly chopped

1 Preheat the oven to 200°C (180°C fan).

2 Place the sweet potatoes on a flat baking tray and bake in the oven for 40 minutes or until tender when pierced with a fork. Remove from the oven, slice in half and allow to cool completely.

3 Scoop the flesh from the sweet potatoes into a large bowl and mash with the back of a fork (discard the skins). Add the ricotta, Parmesan, nutmeg, pepper, thyme leaves and egg and stir until completely smooth. Add the flour and mix until a rough dough comes together.

4 Turn the dough out onto a floured surface, form into a ball and wrap in cling film. Leave to rest in the fridge for 30 minutes and up to 24 hours.

5 Sprinkle a clean work surface with flour and split the chilled dough into three pieces. Roll each one into a long sausage shape about 2cm thick and then cut into 3cm pieces. Roll each one into a rough oval shape and press the top with a floured fork to make a light indent.

6 Bring a large pan of salted water to the boil and add the gnocchi. Cook for 5–6 minutes or until the little dumplings float to the top.

7 While the gnocchi are cooking, place a large frying pan over a medium-high heat and melt half the butter in half the oil. When the butter begins to foam, add half the garlic and sage and fry for 1–2 minutes. Add half the kale and toss to coat. Pour in 3 tablespoons of the gnocchi cooking water, cover with a lid and cook for 3 minutes or until the kale is wilted. Using a slotted spoon, add half the gnocchi to the pan with the kale and toss to coat.

8 Repeat this process again with the remaining ingredients. Serve the gnocchi immediately sprinkled with a little grated Parmesan.

In recent years Ireland has become known as a serious food destination, but as a nation who also knows how to have a good time we still have a few dirty food secrets. Take, for example, the 3-in-1 – an infamous concoction of curry sauce, chips and fried rice – a favourite of late-night Dublin. While I'm not comparing this katsu curry to the 3-in-1, it does have similar qualities: spicy curry sauce and crispy chicken all served with sticky rice. Let's just say it hits the spot, late night or not.

Hands-on time: 50 minutes | **Total time: 1 hour**

CHICKEN KATSU CURRY

SERVES 4

4 chicken breasts (about 150g each)

150ml sunflower oil

1 large free-range egg, beaten

1 tbsp soy sauce

100g Japanese panko breadcrumbs

25g flour, seasoned

300g sticky rice, cooked, to serve

6 spring onions, thinly sliced, to serve

FOR THE CURRY SAUCE

1 tbsp sunflower oil

1 onion, finely chopped

2 garlic cloves, finely chopped

1 thumb-sized piece of fresh ginger, very finely chopped

1 tbsp curry powder

1 tsp ground turmeric

¼ tsp chilli powder

1 tbsp tomato purée

500ml chicken stock

1 tsp cornflour

2 tsp rice wine vinegar

1 tbsp honey

1 tbsp soy sauce

1 First make the sauce. Heat the oil in a pan over a medium heat, add the onion and fry for 6 minutes before stirring in the garlic and ginger; fry for 1–2 minutes. Sprinkle in the curry powder, turmeric, chilli powder and tomato purée and stir to coat the vegetables.

2 Pour in the chicken stock and bring to a steady simmer. Cook for 8 minutes and then mix 2 tablespoons of the hot liquid with the cornflour in a bowl until it is smooth. Pour this back into the pan along with the rice wine vinegar, honey and soy sauce. Cook for a further 3 minutes until the sauce has thickened and then blitz until smooth with a hand-held stick blender.

3 Put the chicken breasts on a chopping board, place a piece of parchment paper on top and, using a rolling pin, bash the breasts to flatten them to a thickness of about 2–3cm.

4 Heat the oil in a large frying pan over a medium-high heat. Whisk together the egg and soy sauce in a deep, flat bowl, and put the breadcrumbs and seasoned flour in separate bowls. Remove the parchment paper and dip each breast first in the seasoned flour, then in the egg mixture and finally the panko breadcrumbs.

5 Fry the crumbed chicken in the oil for 5–6 minutes until golden brown and cooked all the way through. Remove with a slotted spoon and transfer to a plate lined with kitchen paper.

6 Slice the chicken and serve with the cooked sticky rice, spring onions and a generous amount of curry sauce.

While this recipe doesn't quite fit into the quick-cook, 15-minute meal category, I do feel it deserves a little love for its simplicity. It's dishes like this, using ingredients you are bound to have hiding away in the kitchen cupboards, which make for great cooking. Spiced chicken legs sizzle in the oven while all you have to worry about is sticking a few ingredients in a bowl and stirring – kitchen meltdowns be gone! This is my kind of cooking.

Hands-on time: 20 minutes | **Total time: 55 minutes**

SPICE RUB CHICKEN LEG SUPPER

SERVES 4

4 large chicken legs

4 tbsp olive oil

6 long, thin carrots (about 450g), scrubbed and trimmed

1 large red onion, quartered but root left intact

Natural yoghurt, to serve (optional)

FOR THE SPICE RUB

3 tbsp sea salt

2 tbsp ground cumin

2 tbsp smoked paprika

2 tsp ground turmeric

2 tsp cayenne pepper

FOR THE BULGUR

250g bulgur wheat

100g tinned chickpeas, rinsed and drained

50g dried apricots, roughly chopped

50g sultanas

500ml hot chicken stock

Sea salt and freshly ground black pepper

1 Preheat the oven to 200°C (180°C fan).

2 Put the chicken legs into a bowl, pour over half of the oil and all the ingredients for the spice rub. Massage the spices all over the chicken until it's completely coated. (If you have the time cover the bowl with cling film and place in the fridge overnight to allow the flavours to permeate the meat.)

3 Transfer the chicken to a large roasting tray (40 x 30cm) along with the carrots and red onion. Spread everything out on the tray, making sure there is enough space between all the ingredients on the tray for them to cook evenly. Pat some of the spices from the chicken onto the onions and carrots. Drizzle over the remaining oil and roast in the oven for 45 minutes or until the chicken is crisp, golden and cooked through and the carrots are tender.

4 Halfway through the chicken cooking time, start preparing the bulgur. Place the bulgur wheat, chickpeas, apricots and sultanas into a bowl and pour over the hot stock. Stir and cover with cling film, then leave to stand for 20 minutes until the bulgur has soaked up all the liquid. Fluff up with a fork and taste and adjust the seasoning.

5 Serve the chicken on a bed of bulgur with the carrots, red onion and a dollop of natural yoghurt, if you like.

This is a simplified version of my mom's classic Coq Au Vin Blanc, a recipe that continues to be a real family favourite. It's a perfect stovetop supper that requires very little effort. Served with spiky and peppery dressed salad leaves it certainly hits the spot.

Hands-on time: 25 minutes | Total time: 40–45 minutes

WHITE WINE CHICKEN THIGHS WITH FRENCH MUSTARD SALAD

SERVES 4

1 tbsp olive oil

100g pancetta

8 bone-in skin-on chicken thighs

1 large onion, finely chopped

3 garlic cloves, very finely chopped

Small handful of thyme sprigs, leaves picked

100ml white wine

100ml cream

200g mixed leaves, washed and dried

Sea salt and freshly ground black pepper

FOR THE SALAD DRESSING

3 tbsp extra-virgin olive oil

1 tbsp white wine vinegar

1 tsp Dijon mustard

1 tsp honey

1 garlic clove, very finely chopped

1 Heat the oil in a large frying pan (with a lid) over a high heat and brown the pancetta and the chicken thighs on all sides. Transfer to a plate lined with kitchen paper and set aside.

2 Reduce the heat to medium and add the onion. Season with salt and pepper and cook for 6 minutes or until softened. Stir through the garlic and thyme and fry for a further minute. Pour in the white wine and allow to bubble for a minute or so before returning the chicken and pancetta to the pan. Cover with a lid and cook for 20 minutes or until the chicken is cooked all the way through.

3 Remove the lid, lower the heat and stir through the cream; taste and adjust the seasoning. Allow to bubble away for a further 5 minutes until the sauce becomes slightly thicker.

4 Place all the ingredients for the salad dressing in a jar with a tight-fitting lid and shake until combined and emulsified. Put the salad leaves into a mixing bowl, pour the dressing over and toss through until they are completely coated.

5 Serve the chicken with the salad – be sure to spoon over any extra juices from the pan.

Similar to a paella, this one-pan chicken dish provides hearty comfort with each bite – perfect for a relaxed dinner for friends. Short grain rice is a must here; arborio can be found in most supermarkets but look out for the Spanish bomba rice as well.

Hands-on time: 30 minutes | Total time: 50 minutes

ARROZ CON POLLO

SERVES 4

850g chicken thighs, skin on

1 tbsp dried oregano

1–2 tbsp olive oil

2 onions, finely chopped

2 red peppers, deseeded and sliced lengthways

4 garlic cloves, finely chopped

½ tsp dried chilli flakes

75ml white wine

2 x 400g tins plum tomatoes

400ml chicken stock

Generous pinch of saffron

250g short grain rice (arborio or Spanish bomba)

100g green olives, roughly crushed and stones removed

Sea salt and freshly ground black pepper

1 Place the chicken in a bowl and toss with the oregano and a generous amount of sea salt and black pepper; set aside.

2 Place a casserole over a medium-high heat and add 1 tablespoon of the olive oil. Cook the chicken thighs, in batches if necessary, until they have an even golden colour all over and are almost cooked through. Drain on a plate lined with kitchen paper.

3 Add the remaining oil to the pan if required and fry the onions and peppers for 6–8 minutes until just tender. Stir through the garlic and chilli flakes and continue to cook for 1–2 minutes until aromatic.

4 Pour in the wine and simmer for 1–2 minutes before adding the tomatoes, chicken stock, saffron, rice and olives. Bring to a steady simmer and then nestle the chicken thighs in the tomato-rice mixture. Reduce the heat, cover with a lid and simmer gently for 15–20 minutes or until the rice is tender and the chicken is cooked all the way through. Make sure the rice doesn't catch on the bottom of the pan by giving it an occasional stir – depending on the rice you use you may need to top up with a little water if it gets too dry before the rice is cooked.

5 Season to taste with salt and pepper and serve while still warm.

Roast chicken with steamed carrots, crispy roast potatoes, rich gravy and maybe a little stuffing will always be one of my favourite meals. But when I do want something different for the bird a spiced yoghurt marinade is never a bad path to take. This low-fuss dinner really benefits from some marinating time if you have it. Otherwise stick it in the oven as soon as it's prepared and see just how easy it is to get delicious results.

Hands-on time: 30 minutes | **Total time: 1½ hours**

GRILLED INDIAN YOGHURT CHICKEN WITH SPICED VEGETABLES

SERVES 4

1 large onion, thickly sliced

1 small head of cauliflower, broken into florets

4 small carrots, sliced in half lengthways

1 x 1.5kg whole chicken, spatchcocked (see page 38)

Sea salt and freshly ground black pepper

FOR THE MARINADE

3 garlic cloves, very finely chopped

1 thumb-sized piece of fresh ginger, very finely chopped

1 tsp ground cumin

2 tsp ground coriander

2 tsp garam masala

1 tsp cayenne pepper

1 tbsp ground turmeric

250ml natural yoghurt

FOR THE QUINOA

3 cardamom pods

200g quinoa

2 tsp vegetable stock granules

Handful of coriander leaves, roughly chopped

25g toasted flaked almonds

1 Preheat the oven to 200°C (180°C fan) and mix all the ingredients for the marinade together in a small bowl.

2 Lay the vegetables across a large flat baking tray, leaving a little room for the chicken in the centre. Place the chicken on top, slash the chicken legs and breast with a sharp knife and then rub the marinade all over the chicken and the vegetables.

3 Place the chicken in the oven and roast for 1 hour or until the chicken is cooked all the way through and the juices run clear. If the skin begins to catch and blacken too much,

cover with foil and return to the oven.

4 While the chicken is cooking, prepare the quinoa. Bash the cardamom pods with the back of a knife and place them in a medium pan with the quinoa and stock granules. Cover with 500ml boiling water and bring back to the boil, cooking for 10 minutes or until the water has evaporated and the grains are tender. When it's ready use a fork to separate the quinoa and fold in the coriander and almonds.

5 When the chicken is cooked remove from the tray and leave to rest under foil. Tip the bulgur wheat on top of the roasted vegetables and toss through. Cut the chicken into portions and place back on top of the bulgur wheat and vegetables. Serve straight from the tray.

There's something very appealing about a recipe that provides addictive chicken with just six ingredients. The sweet and sticky fish sauce mixture lends a unique saltiness to tender chicken pieces. A dish like this is a welcome addition to a dinner table with salads and greens.

Hands-on time: 25 minutes | Total time: 1 hour and 10 minutes

STICKY FISH SAUCE CHICKEN

SERVES 4

100ml fish sauce

50g sugar

1 red chilli, finely chopped

3 garlic cloves, very finely chopped

Large handful of coriander (leaves and stalks), finely chopped

1 x 1.5kg whole chicken

1 Preheat the oven to 200°C (180°C fan).

2 Place the fish sauce, sugar, chilli, garlic and coriander in a small pan and bring to a simmer until the sugar has dissolved and the sauce has thickened slightly.

3 Spatchcock the chicken. Place the chicken breast-side down on a chopping board and use a sharp knife or kitchen shears to cut down either side of the backbone. Remove the backbone, flip the bird over and then push down hard on the breastbone with the palm of your hand to flatten it out. (Alternatively you can ask your butcher to do this for you.)

4 Place the chicken on a large, flat baking tray and coat completely with half the fish sauce mixture. (At this point the chicken can be covered and left to marinade in the fridge for several hours or overnight for the flavours to permeate the meat.)

5 Cook the chicken for 45 minutes, basting regularly with the remaining fish sauce mixture. If the chicken begins to blacken, cover with foil for the remaining cooking time.

6 Cut the chicken into portions and serve with a fresh green salad.

A fantastic make-ahead dinner, which actually improves in flavour if made in advance – a fact my mother loved and used as a regular excuse if we complained about having the same dinner two days in a row. She was right too. This dish can also be made with small lamb shanks for individual portions. The heady mix of spices with sweet tender meat provides a simple hit of dark comfort.

Hands-on time: 30 minutes | **Total time: 2 hours, plus marinating**

MOROCCAN LAMB STEW

SERVES 4

75g sultanas

75g dried apricots, roughly chopped

700g boneless lamb leg, cut into 2.5cm pieces

2 tbsp olive oil

2 large red onions, chopped

4 garlic cloves, very finely chopped

Large thumb-sized piece of fresh ginger, very finely chopped

1 large butternut squash, peeled and roughly chopped into bite-sized chunks

2 x 400g tins chopped tomatoes

400ml chicken stock

Sea salt and freshly ground black pepper

FOR THE SPICE MIX

2 tsp ground cinnamon

2 tsp ground cumin

6 cardamom pods, roughly bashed

2 tsp ground turmeric

2 tsp ground coriander

2 tsp cayenne pepper

TO SERVE

350g couscous, cooked

Handful of fresh coriander, roughly chopped

Natural yoghurt

1 Add the dried fruit to a small bowl and cover with boiling water – set aside to soak.

2 Combine all the ingredients for the spice mix together in a small bowl. Place the lamb in a mixing bowl and add in half the spice mix, then mix together until the spices coat the lamb. Cover with cling film and leave to marinate in the fridge for at least 1 hour, or overnight.

3 Place a large casserole dish over a medium-high heat. Add a tablespoon of the oil and brown the meat in batches until you have a good colour on all sides. Remove from the pan and transfer to a plate lined with kitchen paper.

4 Reduce the heat slightly and add the remaining oil to the pan. Fry the onions, garlic and ginger for 6–8 minutes until softened. Add the remaining spices and toss to coat the onions, frying for a further minute until they become aromatic.

5 Add the lamb back to the pan with the squash, tinned tomatoes, chicken stock and soaked fruit, along with any soaking liquid left in the bowl. Season with salt and pepper and stir to combine all the ingredients. Lower the heat, place a lid ajar on top and simmer away for 1½ hours or until the meat is tender and the sauce has thickened. Stir every now and then to prevent anything sticking on the bottom of the pan.

6 Serve generous portions of the stew over couscous with a sprinkle of coriander and dollops of yoghurt.

This is traditional Irish comfort food made lighter with a completely untraditional topping of creamy cauliflower champ mash.
This recipe can be made with lamb or beef, or as a vegetarian alternative with lentils and beans.

Hands-on time: 30 minutes | **Total time: 1½ hours**

SHEPHERD'S PIE
WITH CAULIFLOWER
CHAMP MASH

SERVES 4

2 tbsp olive oil

1 large onion, chopped

2–3 medium carrots, chopped

680g lamb mince

2 tbsp tomato purée

1 tbsp each of roughly chopped thyme and parsley

2 tsp Worcestershire sauce

400ml beef or lamb stock

Sea salt and freshly ground black pepper

FOR THE TOPPING

1 large cauliflower, broken into florets

200g half-fat crème fraîche

1 large egg yolk

6 spring onions, thinly sliced

Sea salt and freshly ground black pepper

1 Heat 1 tablespoon of the olive oil in a large frying pan over a medium heat and soften the onion and carrots for 5–6 minutes.

2 Turn up the heat and allow the pan to get really hot before you add the lamb mince. Use a fork to break up the meat and allow it to brown and cook through for 3–4 minutes.

3 Stir through the tomato purée, herbs and Worcestershire sauce until combined and then pour over the stock. Bring to a steady simmer, then partially cover, reduce the heat and cook for 45 minutes. Towards the end of this cooking time preheat the oven to 180°C (160°C fan).

4 For the cauliflower mash topping, place the cauliflower in a food processor and blitz until it becomes the texture of couscous. Add the crème fraîche and egg yolk and blitz again to bring the mixture together. Transfer to a bowl, add the spring onions and season with salt and pepper, stirring to combine.

5 When the lamb is ready, season with salt and pepper and transfer to an ovenproof baking dish. Top with the cauliflower champ mash, using a spoon to create a nice finish. Give the topping an extra sprinkle of ground black pepper and bake in the oven for 25 minutes until the top is starting to brown and the mince is bubbling up around the edges. Serve straight away for a delicious and comforting supper!

SWEET
SNACKS

———

Strawberry Fool

———

Instant Mango Sorbet

———

Mushed Raspberries with Ricotta and Pistachios

———

Exotic Fruit Salad with Lime and Mint Syrup

———

Instant Banana and Chocolate Chip Ice Cream

———

Raspberry and Yoghurt Panna Cotta

———

Chocolate Hazelnut Newtella

———

Baked Stone Fruit Salad

———

Chocolate and Peanut Butter Banana Bread

———

5-Ingredient Chocolate Chip Cookies

———

Chocolate and Raspberry Devil Cake

———

Quinoa Chocolate Cake with Avocado Frosting

———

Oaty Rhubarb Crumble Cake

———

I, for one, always have room for dessert. In fact if it's not on the table after a good dinner, I do feel somewhat hard done by. I'm not looking for a stonking slice of chocolate cake every day, but on special occasions it's just something that finishes a meal off nicely and appropriately shifts gear. Baking was the first thing I turned my hand to when I started cooking; as far as my mum was concerned it was an easy option, with fewer hot pans and sharp knives to worry about. While I like to think I've stepped it up from the shortbread jam biscuits I used to make growing up, the gratification from mixing a simple batter in a bowl and seeing it come out of the oven as something spectacular doesn't go away.

Some of the recipes in this chapter (like the rich Chocolate and Raspberry Devil Cake, Chocolate and Peanut Butter Banana Bread or Oaty Rhubarb Crumble Cake) are all about complete and utter indulgence. Some give a nod to the somewhat cleaner eating habits I've picked up along the way – although take one look at the chocolate cake on page 97 and you would never guess avocado and quinoa were the key ingredients. While a few of the desserts are an ode to speedy sweet solutions, like Instant Mango Sorbet and Instant Banana and Chocolate Chip Ice Cream, both of which can be whizzed up in an instant, most of the recipes in this chapter take just minutes to prepare, from the 5-Ingredient Chocolate Chip Cookies to the mouth-watering Baked Stone Fruit Salad.

Any good home cook needs an arsenal of quick-to-prepare dessert recipes. Here is a perfect dish to add to your collection – four ingredients brought together to celebrate one of my favourite summer fruits. This somewhat lighter version is made with Greek yoghurt rather than whipped cream. Serve with shortbread biscuits.

Hands-on time: 5 minutes | Total time: 5 minutes, plus chilling

STRAWBERRY FOOL

SERVES 4

350g strawberries, plus extra to decorate

2 tbsp icing sugar, sifted

500g Greek yoghurt

2 tsp vanilla bean paste

1 Roughly chop the strawberries and add to a bowl with 1 tablespoon of the icing sugar. Mash roughly with a fork until you have a chunky mixture.

2 In a separate bowl, mix together the Greek yoghurt, remaining icing sugar and vanilla bean paste. Fold the strawberry mush through the Greek yoghurt.

3 Transfer to individual serving glasses and chill in the fridge until ready to serve, decorated with a few fresh strawberries.

The instant in the title is no exaggeration. This sorbet can be made with minimum effort and serious results. Serve it as a light and refreshing dessert.

Hands-on time: 5 minutes | Total time: 5 minutes, plus freezing

INSTANT MANGO SORBET

SERVES 4

3 large mangoes

1 ripe banana, peeled

Zest and juice of 2 limes

1 Peel the mangoes and cut the flesh into chunks. Cut the banana into chunks and spread out on a tray. Place in the freezer for at least 4 hours or overnight if possible.

2 Place the frozen mango and banana into a food processor with the lime zest and juice. Blitz on high until the mixture is the consistency of a thick sorbet (you can add a couple of tablespoons of ice-cold water if the consistency looks too thick).

3 Transfer to individual serving glasses and eat straight away.

Dessert in an instant with minimal effort – music to my ears! Made with the ripest raspberries and freshest ricotta this is a true summer indulgence. The inspiration comes from late summer evenings in my wife Sofie's native Sweden. Raspberries grow wild in the hedgerows there and if you can stop the locals from nabbing them before you do, the thing is to enjoy them simply with creamy ricotta and honey.

Hands-on time: 10 minutes | Total time: 10 minutes

MUSHED RASPBERRIES WITH RICOTTA AND PISTACHIOS

SERVES 4

300g raspberries

400g ricotta

100ml double cream, whipped to soft peaks

3 tbsp honey, plus extra for drizzling

Generous glug of Cointreau, or other orange liqueur

50g pistachios, shelled and finely blitzed

1 Place half the raspberries in a small bowl and mash with the back of a fork.

2 Tip the ricotta into a bowl and beat with a wooden spoon until just smooth. Fold through the whipped cream, mashed raspberries, honey and Cointreau.

3 Pile generous spoonfuls of the raspberry ricotta mix into small serving bowls and top with the remaining raspberries, a sprinkle of pistachios and a final drizzle of honey.

There is something instantly exotic about a pineapple; it gives any fruit bowl a glamorous facelift, brings retro charm to cakes and with very little preparation you can create something delicious with it. This quick dessert will be a testament to your knife skills, as it's best made with very thinly sliced fruit. Don't skimp on the mint, it pairs beautifully with sweet pineapple.

Hands-on time: 10 minutes | Total time: 10 minutes

EXOTIC FRUIT SALAD
WITH LIME AND MINT SYRUP

SERVES 4

1 large pineapple, peeled, cored and very thinly sliced

1 large mango, peeled and very thinly sliced

125g blueberries

Small handful of fresh mint, thinly sliced

FOR THE SYRUP

5 tbsp soft dark brown sugar

Zest and juice of 2 limes

1 Put the sugar, lime zest and juice in a small pan with 100ml water. Heat gently until the sugar has dissolved and bring to a gentle simmer until you have a syrup. Remove from the heat and allow to cool slightly.

2 Arrange the sliced pineapple, mango and blueberries on a serving platter and spoon over the syrup. Sprinkle with the sliced mint and serve.

What can I say? I'm in love! I never imagined I would ever suggest this as a recipe but frozen bananas and smooth peanut butter laced with dark chocolate is a thing of beauty. Creamy, smooth and an instant sweet hit, this is well worth trying. Next time you have bananas going black in the fruit bowl, peel them, stick them in a resealable bag and freeze for a recipe like this – I guarantee you will be surprised by the results.

Hands-on time: 5 minutes | **Total time: 20 minutes**

INSTANT BANANA
AND CHOCOLATE CHIP
ICE CREAM

SERVES 2

4 frozen bananas

3 tbsp smooth peanut butter

75g good-quality dark chocolate, chopped into rough chunks

1 Remove the bananas from the freezer and allow to defrost for 15 minutes.

2 Place the bananas and peanut butter in a food processor and blend for about 2 minutes until smooth and creamy. The mixture will start off crumbly but stop and start the processor a few times, scraping down the sides in between and you will be left with some creamy magic!

3 Transfer the ice cream to a bowl and use a spatula to fold through the dark chocolate chunks.

4 Serve straight away with extra chocolate sprinkled over the top or cover and freeze until needed. This will keep in the freezer for 1 month.

The true brilliance of a panna cotta is just how fancy it seems to those who haven't made it. A perfect dome of vanilla-scented crème makes it the perfect base for whatever fruit is in season. This variation uses yoghurt, which makes the dessert somewhat lighter and, of course, the raspberries can be replaced with blueberries, strawberries, or rhubarb – just adjust the sweetness to your liking.

Hands-on time: 15 minutes | **Total time: 20 minutes, plus chilling**

RASPBERRY AND YOGHURT PANNA COTTA

SERVES 4

FOR THE PANNA COTTA

300g single cream

75g caster sugar

2 vanilla pods, split and seeds scraped (or 1 tsp vanilla bean paste)

10g leaf gelatine

250g natural yoghurt

Mint sprigs, to decorate

FOR THE BERRY SAUCE

300g raspberries

2 tbsp caster sugar

Splash of crème de cassis (optional)

1 Place the cream, sugar, vanilla pods and seeds in a pan over a medium heat and bring to a gentle simmer. Stir until the sugar has dissolved, then remove from the heat and leave to infuse.

2 Meanwhile, place the gelatine sheets in a small bowl and cover with a little water. Leave to stand for 5 minutes until the gelatine has softened. Remove the softened gelatine from the bowl and squeeze out any excess water.

3 Remove the vanilla pods from the warmed cream, then add the softened gelatine and yoghurt and stir through until dissolved. Divide the mixture between four serving glasses, cover with cling film and place in the fridge to set for at least 3 hours or overnight.

4 To prepare the berry sauce, place all the ingredients (reserving about a quarter of the raspberries) in a small pan and place over a medium-high heat. Bring to the boil, mashing the raspberries with the back of the spoon and stirring occasionally. Reduce and simmer for a few minutes until slightly thickened. Blitz until smooth with a hand-held stick blender and then pass through a sieve to remove the seeds. Stir through the reserved raspberries.

5 Serve each panna cotta with a few tablespoons of the berry sauce and decorate with a mint sprig.

While I'm slightly opposed to the idea that when following a healthy diet you have to replace sugary snacks with miserable alternatives, I do have a soft spot for this very easy to make chocolate spread!

Hands-on time: 15 minutes | Total time: 25 minutes

CHOCOLATE HAZELNUT NEWTELLA

MAKES 550G

350g hazelnuts

100g maple syrup

4 tbsp raw cacao powder

2 tsp vanilla extract

½ tsp sea salt

1 Preheat the oven to 180°C (160°C fan).

2 Tip the nuts onto a large baking tray and roast for 8–10 minutes or until toasted and golden. Allow the nuts to cool slightly before pouring them onto a clean, dry tea towel and wrapping up. Roll the nuts in the tea towel until their skins are loosened and can be removed easily.

3 Transfer the skinned nuts to a food processor and blend for about 6 minutes until you have a thick, creamy nut butter, scraping down the sides as you go.

4 Add in the remaining ingredients and 75ml water. Blend until you have a smooth mixture. Transfer to a lidded jar and hey presto, healthy homemade chocolate spread! This will keep in the fridge for up to 3 weeks.

A late summer evening's dessert that instantly reminds me of time spent in the South of France. While staying just outside Cannes, we made a visit to Marché Forville, a covered fresh produce market, filled with stunning displays of cured meats, French cheeses and locally grown fruit and vegetables. When I travel I often regret not having a kitchen to make use of the ingredients I come across but this time I was able to create this simple treat of a dessert, late one evening. If you want to go the extra mile, arrange the fruit across a sheet of puff pastry and fold in the edges, to make a rough galette.

Hands-on time: 5 minutes | Total time: 50 minutes

BAKED STONE FRUIT SALAD

SERVES 4

25g coconut sugar

Zest and juice of 1 lime

1 vanilla pod, split lengthways and seeds scraped out

4 peaches, halved and stoned

6 apricots, halved and stoned

3 nectarines, quartered and stoned

Vanilla yoghurt, to serve

25g flaked almonds, toasted

1 Preheat the oven to 220°C (200°C fan).

2 In a bowl mix together the coconut sugar, lime zest and juice and vanilla seeds until well combined.

3 Place all the fruits in an ovenproof baking dish and toss with the sugar mixture. Bake in the oven for 45 minutes or until the fruit is just tender.

4 Serve the fruit with a dollop of yoghurt and some toasted flaked almonds.

Warning! The following recipe is extremely addictive! Moist banana bread with its faintly exotic flavour is delicious by itself, cut in thick, generous slices. But add chocolate and peanut butter to the mix and you are guaranteed to finish the whole loaf!

Hands-on time: 15 minutes | Total time: 1¼ hours

CHOCOLATE AND PEANUT BUTTER BANANA BREAD

MAKES 1 LOAF

125g butter, plus extra for greasing

200g caster sugar

2 large free-range eggs

200g plain flour

1 tsp bicarbonate of soda

3 large ripe bananas

1 tsp vanilla extract

100g good-quality dark chocolate chips

75g smooth peanut butter, slightly warmed

1 Preheat the oven to 180°C (160°C fan) and grease and line a 900g loaf tin with parchment paper.

2 Cream the butter and sugar together in a bowl with a hand-held electric mixer until light and pale.

3 Add one egg and a little flour and mix through, then repeat with the other egg, remaining flour and bicarbonate of soda until everything is mixed through and smooth.

4 Mash the bananas with the back of a fork. Add them to the bowl with the vanilla extract and chocolate chips and mix through.

5 Pour the mixture into the loaf tin and then place dollops of the peanut butter across the top. Using a skewer, swirl the peanut butter through the batter and then bake in the oven for about 1 hour. Check on it after 25 minutes – if it looks like it is browning too much, cover the top with foil and return to the oven. It is cooked when a metal skewer inserted into the centre of the loaf comes out clean.

6 Allow to cool for a few minutes in the tin and then remove and place on a wire rack to cool completely.

I am eternally drawn to recipes that have just five ingredients and are easy to remember, especially if they result in slightly addictive cookies like these ones. Play around with the core flavours as you wish, white chocolate, raisins and nuts are all welcome additions.

Hands-on time: 8 minutes | Total time: 18–20 minutes

5-INGREDIENT CHOCOLATE CHIP COOKIES

MAKES 12

1 large free-range egg

150g peanut butter

50g honey

50g rolled oats

50g dark chocolate chips

1 Preheat the oven to 180°C (160°C fan) and line a large baking tray with parchment paper.

2 Place all the ingredients in a bowl and mix together until you have a smooth dough.

3 Place tablespoons of the dough on to the baking tray. Bake in the oven for 10–12 minutes until firm to the touch. Allow to cool on the baking tray before eating.

A gluten-free chocolate cake I come back to time and time again, made even more irresistible with a topping of delicate, jewel-like raspberries.

Hands-on time: 40 minutes | **Total time: 1 hour**

CHOCOLATE AND RASPBERRY DEVIL CAKE

SERVES 8

225g dark chocolate (70% cocoa solids), finely chopped

125g butter, diced

175g caster sugar

1 tsp vanilla extract

100g ground almonds

6 large eggs, separated

250g raspberries

Chocolate curls, to decorate

FOR THE GLAZE

100g dark chocolate (70% cocoa solids), finely chopped

30g butter

50g icing sugar, sifted

75ml cream

1 Preheat the oven to 180°C (160°C fan) and grease and line two 20cm spring-form cake tins with parchment paper.

2 Melt the chocolate and butter together in a large heatproof bowl set over a pan of barely simmering water.

3 Remove the bowl from the heat and mix in the sugar, vanilla extract and ground almonds with a spatula. Stir through the egg yolks, one at a time, mixing after each addition, until you have a thick batter.

4 Put the egg whites in the bowl of a free-standing mixer (or use a hand-held electric mixer) and whisk the egg whites until stiff peaks form. Add the egg whites to the chocolate batter and fold through gently until just combined.

5 Divide the chocolate batter between the prepared cake tins and bake in the oven for about 20 minutes until firm but with a slight wobble in the centre. Remove the cakes from the oven and allow to sit on a wire rack to cool in the tin for a few minutes before removing from the tins to cool completely.

6 Meanwhile, make the glaze. Melt the chocolate and butter in a heatproof bowl set over a pan of barely simmering water. When melted, remove from the heat and whisk in the icing sugar and cream, a little bit at a time. Allow to cool until the mixture becomes thick enough to leave a figure of eight on the surface.

7 Place one of the cakes on a cake stand and spread half the glaze across the surface. Arrange half the raspberries over the surface and then place the second cake layer on top. Spread the remaining glaze across the top and decorate with the remaining raspberries. Finish with chocolate curls.

Don't reveal the title of this cake or the ingredients used in it and see if your friends can guess – it's nearly impossible to tell that the rich sponge gets it's moistness from quinoa or its luscious frosting from avocado. A slightly healthier take on a classic chocolate cake.

Hands-on time: 20 minutes | Total time: 1 hour

QUINOA CHOCOLATE CAKE WITH AVOCADO FROSTING

SERVES 8

150g cooked quinoa

4 large free-range eggs

50ml milk

150g butter, cubed

1 tsp vanilla extract

200g coconut sugar

100g cocoa powder

1 tsp baking powder

½ tsp bicarbonate of soda

FOR THE CHOCOLATE AVOCADO FROSTING

2 ripe avocados, stoned and flesh scooped out

75g cocoa powder

1 tsp espresso powder

75g maple syrup

1 tsp vanilla extract

½ tsp sea salt

1 Preheat the oven to 180°C (160°C fan) and grease and line a 20cm spring-form cake tin with parchment paper.

2 Place the quinoa, eggs, milk, butter and vanilla extract in a food processor and blitz until smooth. Add the coconut sugar, cocoa powder, baking powder and bicarbonate of soda and blitz again to combine. Transfer the mixture to the prepared tin and bake for 35–40 minutes or until a skewer comes out clean.

3 Remove from the oven and allow to cool slightly before removing from the tin and setting on a wire rack to cool completely.

4 For the frosting, place the avocados, cocoa powder, espresso powder, maple syrup, vanilla extract and sea salt in a food processor and blitz until smooth, scraping down the sides of the bowl as necessary. Use a spatula to spread over the top of the cooled cake and dig in.

I make a variation of this cake with apples but if you can get your hands on some young pink rhubarb, this is one of the best ways to show it off.

Hands-on time: 30 minutes | **Total time: 1¾ hours**

OATY RHUBARB CRUMBLE CAKE

SERVES 6–8

FOR THE CAKE

100g butter, plus extra for greasing

150g soft light brown sugar

2 large free-range eggs

75ml milk

200g plain flour, sifted

1 tsp baking powder

Pinch of salt

1 tsp ground cinnamon

300g rhubarb, trimmed and finely sliced

Single cream, to serve

FOR THE CRUMBLE TOPPING

150g plain flour

150g jumbo rolled oats

175g soft light brown sugar

200g cold butter, cut into pieces

Icing sugar, to dust (optional)

1 Preheat the oven to 180°C (160°C fan) and grease and line a 20cm spring-form cake tin with parchment paper.

2 With a hand-held electric mixer, beat the butter and sugar in a large bowl until pale and fluffy. Add the eggs, one at a time, mixing until they are incorporated. Mix in the milk and then fold through the flour, baking powder, salt and cinnamon until you have a thick cake batter.

3 Pour the batter into the prepared tin, using a spatula to spread across the base of the tin. Arrange the rhubarb across the top leaving a gap of 2cm around the edges.

4 For the crumble topping, place the flour, oats, sugar and butter in a large bowl. Using your fingertips, rub all the ingredients together until it resembles chunky breadcrumbs. Sprinkle the crumble topping on top of the batter.

5 Bake in the oven for 1 hour 10 minutes or until a skewer inserted into the centre comes out clean. Leave to cool for a few minutes in the tin before removing, and dust with icing sugar (if using). Cut the cake into slices and serve with cream.

LIVE

Being Irish and writing about 'finding balance in life' or 'focusing on positivity' can't really be done without inviting a raised eyebrow or a roll of the eyes. It just doesn't come as naturally to us as our spiritual American cousins. We are a cynical bunch, the Irish, but while we may more often than not find ourselves discussing the weather rather than how we really feel, for me the last few years have been filled with meditation, yoga and (gasp) green juices! Finding balance is something I have always struggled with due to the nature of the work I do. Every day is different, which means it's difficult to create a regular routine, which in turn results in huge highs and inconsistent lows.

A few years ago I spent time learning from Tal Ben Shahar, a leading positive psychology author who writes: 'Attaining lasting happiness requires that we enjoy the journey on our way toward a destination we deem valuable. Happiness is not about making it to the peak of the mountain nor is it about climbing aimlessly around the mountain; happiness is the experience of climbing toward the peak.' Many of us spend our lives striving for that golden moment, that perfect place in life where work, relationships, diet, fitness and happiness are all aligned. Over the years I've come to the conclusion that striking that balance is more about putting in place a continuous process of maintenance, something that requires regular check-ups. Now I do understand that that might sound like work in itself – if you're struggling to keep any one of those life aspects in check the whole idea of adding emotional maintenance to your to-do list might seem a challenge too far. However it is manageable with the introduction of some positive habits.

The thing that always amazes me about all this positive psychology is that most of it is stuff we already know but hardly ever put into practise. How many of us have read one of those '10 steps to happiness' articles, resolved to make certain changes and then found ourselves falling back into the same old habits? Aside from the food I eat, finding routines and good habits that I can control has become increasingly important in my day-to-day life. This might sound obvious but one of the biggest changes for me has been getting out of bed an hour or so before I need to,

allowing me time for non-work activities. Like many of us I had been stumbling out of bed with only minutes to spare and getting straight to work without paying any attention to the things that could significantly improve the way my day would turn out. Creating a morning routine that was meaningful and productive was a real turning point for me. Essentially it boils down to exercise, getting outdoors, eating a healthy breakfast where possible, including time for meditation and time to write out my plan for the day. It's about choosing to take control of the day rather than the day taking control of me.

Once I've applied my perfect morning habits, by the time it comes to actually getting down to work, I find myself happier, more productive and far more focused. I'm as strict about this routine as I can be but I also don't beat myself up if I don't get everything on the list ticked off. Sometimes there is only time for 15 minutes of deep breathing and focusing on the day ahead; sometimes it's just a case of making sure I have a really nutritious breakfast. The most important thing for me is having a strong road map for the day.

In terms of exercise, you might be able to tell by my spaghetti arms that I am by no means a gym bunny. However, I do love to be active and outdoors and I fully appreciate the benefits exercise has to the immune system. Despite trying many forms of exercise over the last few years, the one thing I come back to is yoga as it's something I can do wherever I

am, using online classes to practise. I am certainly not a fully-fledged yogi but I find it helps me relax, unwind, energise, reset and refocus. If I'm really 'on it' I also add running to the mix but I'm more likely to spend some of my 'outdoor' time going on a hike with Sofie and our dog Max – something we're well used to after years of pounding the paths around the cliffs close by our house.

'Flow' is a word that is used quite often these days and refers to that moment of being in the zone, when you are fully focused on an activity you enjoy which in turn energises you. However, 'restoration' is also a key aspect of maintaining balance in what I do. For a long time I had been finding myself in a position where one project merged right into the next without any breathing space. This would leave me completely overwhelmed and exhausted. Now as part of my daily, weekly and monthly plans I work in times for restoration. It's about making time for myself and taking time to do whatever I enjoy. It can be as simple as reading a book or taking the dog for a walk, but whatever activity it is, it needs to be something completely absorbing and something that I thoroughly look forward to. It also means no phone, no email and basically no distraction – like most people I find this quite difficult to do.

The bottom line here is that these are things that I have found to work for me and so it's important to find things that work for you in the search for maintaining balance and

happiness. That maintenance in my world of course has a strong focus on the types of food I eat. As a food lover, I rarely say no to trying something new or downright indulgent, whatever the calorific content. But this seemingly carefree attitude does come with a need to be mindful and so I do pack my diet with as much fresh fruit and vegetables, grains and pulses as I possibly can. (Something's got to balance out all the chocolate lava cakes, right?) I hold my hands up to being part of the green juice brigade, the quinoa massive and the spirulina squad but I do so with strong ties to the food I grew up with. It's important to maintain equilibrium between the two, while always striving for grub that tastes great – something that's not always high on the agenda with our hard core 'clean eating' friends.

The recipes in this chapter are the types of food I include in my diet to up the nutrition content, but always with a flavour in mind. Food that tastes great but is also good for you can be a tricky balance to strike and I tend to rely on spices and aromatic elements to elevate many of my healthier focused dishes. Middle Eastern and Indian spices and pastes, vibrant South East Asian flavours combined with nutritious and healthy ingredients make for some seriously great food which can easily be added to your daily kitchen routine.

GET UP
AND GO

———

Ultimate Green Smoothie

———

Bircher Muesli with Honey Yoghurt

———

Super Fruit Smoothie Bowl

———

Turmeric, Ginger and Cayenne Power Juice

———

Tropical Fruit Balls

———

Baked Apple Porridge

———

Scandi Quinoa Breakfast Bowl

———

Oatmeal Muffin Cups

———

Super Green Omelette

———

Hot Smoked Salmon with Avocado Smash on Toast

———

I have always been a morning person. Some may suggest annoyingly so, but I get my best work done right after breakfast and with my newly formed habit of early starts I've been enjoying those early hours all the more. A huge part of my morning routine is eating a solid breakfast; an early start requires food that's going to keep me going.

I absolutely love cooking a leisurely brunch when I have time, but a quick breakfast that is merely fuel is not something that has ever inspired me to eat in the morning. First thing in the morning is when we need food the most, as the time we spend asleep is the longest period we go without eating – surely that means we should wake up ready for a serious feed? I've learned that it doesn't always work that way but there are ways to get around those picky morning habits.

I can't promise that the recipes in this chapter will solve all your breakfast woes, but added to your weekday routine they certainly have the potential to. In my case I have to make things interesting. Smoothie bowls, bite-sized fruit energy balls, green omelettes and baked porridge might sound a tad over the top, but they are just some of the simple, easy-to-make and inventive ways I try and get myself to eat a decent breakfast. They do the job for me, so give them a go!

Green smoothies can be tricky to master – get the balance of sweetness and bitterness wrong and you're in for a whole world of pain. A recent visit to Green Beards juice shop in Ranelagh, Dublin provided the inspiration for this one, which is easily the best I have tried. Add whatever other vegetables (spinach or broccoli works well) you fancy but don't skimp on the medjool dates as they add a vital sweet toffee taste. Freezing bananas is a great way to use up any uneaten bananas knocking around in your fruit bowl – just peel and roughly chop before freezing.

Hands-on time: 2 minutes | **Total time: 2 minutes**

ULTIMATE GREEN SMOOTHIE

SERVES 2

1 frozen banana

750ml unsweetened almond milk

1 tbsp chia seeds

1 tbsp matcha green tea powder

4 kale stalks

½ ripe avocado

5 medjool dates, pitted

1 Add all the ingredients to a high-speed blender and blitz until you're left with a smoothie consistency.

2 If you find the mixture is too thick add a little water until you have a pourable consistency. Pour into glasses and serve.

As a kid the idea of cold oats soaked in milk never really appealed to me but as I am now an avid porridge fan, I am keen to find variations. This version is great to prepare the night before and you can enjoy it with whatever berries, nuts or seeds take your fancy. It's also delicious served with yoghurt and rhubarb compote.

Hands-on time: 5 minutes | **Total time: 5 minutes, plus resting**

BIRCHER MUESLI
WITH HONEY YOGHURT

SERVES 2

100g rolled oats

1 heaped tbsp chia seeds

350ml milk

1 ripe banana, mashed

1 tbsp honey

TOPPING IDEAS

4 tbsp natural yoghurt

2 tbsp honey

125g raspberries

125g blueberries

2 tbsp sunflower seeds, toasted

1–2 tbsp sesame seeds, toasted

1 In a bowl mix together the rolled oats, chia seeds, milk, banana and honey. Cover and leave to sit in the fridge overnight.

2 When you are ready to serve, scoop into two serving bowls. Dollop with yoghurt, drizzle with honey and scatter with berries and seeds.

SUPER FRUIT SMOOTHIE BOWL

When I can't face another bowl of porridge, a smoothie is my go-to breakfast. Recently I've been drawn to these smoothie bowls, which litter Pinterest, Instagram and Facebook. The smoothie base here can be frozen and scooped like ice cream as I enjoyed recently, making it almost feel like dessert for breakfast!

Hands-on time: 5 minutes | Total time: 5 minutes

SERVES 2

FOR THE SMOOTHIE BASE

2 ripe bananas, sliced and frozen

350g frozen mixed berries

½ avocado

Small handful of baby spinach leaves

25g porridge oats

500ml unsweetened almond milk

2 tbsp chia seeds

2 tbsp honey

TOPPING IDEAS

Toasted sunflower seeds

Granola

Desiccated coconut

Fresh berries

Toasted nuts (almonds, pecan nuts, walnuts)

1 Place all the ingredients for the smoothie base into a food processor and blitz until completely smooth. Pour into two deep bowls.

2 Time to get creative! Decorate the top with as many of the suggested toppings you wish. Serve immediately.

TURMERIC, GINGER AND CAYENNE POWER JUICE

Turmeric's immune-boosting properties have been known for many years but it's having somewhat of a revival recently. Rightly so – apart from its health benefits it adds superb colour and an earthy, sweet flavour to any dish it's used in. Fresh turmeric root can be found in most Asian markets and speciality food stores, but if you can't find it, replace with a teaspoon of the dried stuff.

Hands-on time: 3 minutes | Total time: 3 minutes

SERVES 1

Small thumb-sized piece of fresh turmeric

Small thumb-sized piece of fresh ginger

½ tsp cayenne pepper

½ cucumber

1 celery stick

Thick slice of lemon

Coconut water (optional)

1 Put the turmeric, ginger, cayenne, cucumber, celery and lemon slice in a juicer and juice all until you have a bright coloured juice.

2 If you find the juice too astringent add a splash or two of coconut water to mellow the flavour.

Energy balls have well and truly done the rounds at this stage but they are still a regular fixture in my house. I normally make cocoa and espresso spiked ones but these sweeter tropical balls are just as delicious and are now my new favourite version. They freeze extremely well in a resealable bag but will also keep in the fridge for at least a week.

Hands-on time: 10 minutes | Total time: 1 hour 10 minutes

TROPICAL FRUIT BALLS

MAKES 16 BALLS

125g dried mango

100g dried apricots

75g desiccated coconut

Zest and juice of 1 lime

1 tbsp finely grated fresh ginger

2 tbsp chia seeds

50g porridge oats

4 tbsp coconut oil

Pinch of sea salt

1 Place all the ingredients in a food processor and blitz until you have a smooth mixture that begins to come together.

2 Form the mixture into small balls about the size of a walnut. Place on a plate, cover and chill in the fridge for 1 hour. Eat straight away or store in an airtight container in the fridge for up to 5 days.

I love the idea of warm baked porridge scented with cinnamon and served to the table steaming with a drizzle of honey. I realise this description makes it sound like a cheesy breakfast cereal commercial but in reality this porridge really does deliver!

Hands-on time: 5 minutes | Total time: 30 minutes

BAKED APPLE PORRIDGE

SERVES 2

150g rolled oats

Pinch of salt

550ml water

½ tsp ground cinnamon

3 tbsp honey

Large handful of pecan nuts, roughly chopped

1 large apple, grated, plus extra for garnish

3 tbsp soft dark brown sugar

2 tbsp Greek-style yoghurt, to serve

1 Preheat the oven to 220°C (200°C fan).

2 Place the oats, salt and water in a small pan and bring to a steady simmer over a medium-high heat. Cook for 4–5 minutes or until the porridge oats are softened, stirring constantly.

3 Stir through the cinnamon, honey, nuts and grated apple and then pour into a small (12.5 x 20cm) ovenproof dish. Sprinkle with the brown sugar and place in the oven for 20 minutes until the top is set and golden brown.

4 Serve with a good dollop of yoghurt and some extra apple.

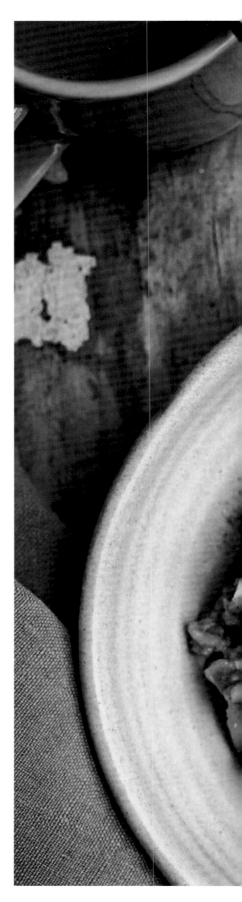

This should technically be called a Scandi 'inspired' breakfast bowl because most of the Scandinavians I know would look sideways at you if you served boiled eggs and salmon with quinoa. But please bear with me: these classic and clean-tasting Scandinavian flavours work incredibly well in a hearty quinoa bowl like this – you might even convince a few Scandis along the way!

Hands-on time: 10 minutes | Total time: 15 minutes

SCANDI QUINOA BREAKFAST BOWL

SERVES 2

2 large free-range eggs

100g quinoa, cooked

Juice of ½ lemon

Large handful of dill, roughly chopped, plus extra to serve

150g sliced smoked salmon

2 tbsp trout roe (optional)

2 radishes, thinly sliced

1 avocado, thinly sliced

Sea salt and freshly ground black pepper

FOR THE HORSERADISH CREAM

4 tbsp soured cream

1 tsp finely grated fresh horseradish

1 tbsp lemon juice

Sea salt and freshly ground black pepper

1 Place the eggs in a pan of cold water and bring to a rolling boil. Turn off the heat, cover with a lid and leave to sit for 4 minutes. Transfer the eggs to a bowl of iced water and allow to cool for a minute or so. Peel the eggs and slice in half.

2 Mix the quinoa with the lemon juice and all but a tablespoon of the chopped dill until evenly combined.

3 Mix together the ingredients for the horseradish cream, add the reserved dill and season to taste.

4 Assemble the bowls: place the quinoa at the bottom and top with the smoked salmon, egg halves, trout roe, if using, radishes and avocado. Add a good dollop of the horseradish cream and a generous sprinkle of chopped dill. Squeeze over a little more lemon juice and sprinkle with black pepper to serve.

See these oatmeal muffin cups as a hybrid between a breakfast muffin and a bowl of porridge – something that can be munched on the go, providing slow-release energy and substance. If you do have the time, enjoy them warm from the oven with yoghurt, honey and fresh fruit.

Hands-on time: 10 minutes | **Total time: 35 minutes**

OATMEAL MUFFIN CUPS

MAKES 10

Coconut oil, for greasing

200g rolled oats

1 tsp ground cinnamon

1 tsp ground cardamom

Pinch of sea salt

1 tsp baking powder

4 tbsp mixed seeds (chia, pumpkin, sesame)

50g raisins

1 ripe banana

1 large free-range egg

3 tbsp almond butter

400ml unsweetened almond milk

4 tbsp maple syrup, plus extra to serve

TO SERVE

Coconut yoghurt

Fresh blueberries and raspberries

1 Preheat the oven to 180°C (160°C fan) and grease a 12-hole muffin tray with coconut oil (you'll only need to grease 10 holes). You could also use paper cases.

2 Place all the dry ingredients in a large bowl and mix until evenly combined.

3 In a mixing jug, mash the banana until smooth, then add the egg and almond butter and whisk together until combined. Slowly pour in the almond milk and maple syrup, whisking until completely incorporated.

4 Pour the wet ingredients into the dry and mix until just combined. Transfer the rough batter into ten of the muffin wells and bake in the oven for 25 minutes until just risen and no longer wet.

5 Serve warm from the oven with yoghurt and fresh berries.

My inner Dr Seuss fan gets excited at the mere thought of green eggs – even without the ham! I often make neon green spinach crêpes filled with Gruyère cheese and ham as a means to satisfy my needs but I do have a slightly lighter alternative in this super green omelette, which can easily become the vehicle for plenty of other ingredients of your choosing.

Hands-on time: 20 minutes | Total time: 20 minutes

SUPER GREEN OMELETTE

SERVES 2

50g baby spinach

Large handful of chives

Large handful of flat-leaf parsley

75ml milk

4 large free-range eggs

1 tbsp sunflower oil

75g sun blushed tomatoes

50g pine nuts, toasted

1 large ripe avocado

100g rindless goats' cheese, crumbled

Sea salt and freshly ground black pepper

1 Place the spinach, chives, parsley and milk in a food processor and blitz until smooth (you may need to scrape down the greens with a spatula halfway through the process).

2 Add the eggs and blitz again to combine, then season with salt and pepper.

3 Heat half the oil in a frying pan over a medium-high heat and pour in half the mixture. Tilt the pan until the mixture completely covers the base. Cook for 2 minutes until just set underneath and then add half the tomatoes, pine nuts, avocado and goats' cheese. Fold the omelette in half and then cook for a further 2 minutes.

4 Repeat with the remaining mixture to make a second omelette.

5 Serve the omelettes hot from the pan or allow to cool and chop up for a lunchbox on-the-go.

There must be a reason why mushy food is comforting in the morning. Perhaps it's a throwback to our time spent being weaned on to real food or fleeting memories of warmth on cold, dark mornings. Either way I'm drawn to anything that can be smashed, mushed or pressed onto a warm, crispy chewy vessel like a toasted bagel or slice of good sourdough. This ideal breakfast/lunch/dinner/midnight snack delivers a creamy, salty, crispy and smooth bite all in one mouthful. Oh and please, the eggs MUST be soft-boiled and served warm for complete satisfaction.

Hands-on time: 4 minutes | Total time: 6 minutes

HOT SMOKED SALMON
WITH AVOCADO SMASH
ON TOAST

SERVES 1

1 large free-range egg

½ large ripe avocado

Squeeze of lemon juice

1 large slice of sourdough bread

2 slices of hot smoked salmon

Few snipped chives

Sea salt and freshly ground black pepper

1 Place the eggs in a pan of cold water and bring to a rolling boil. Turn off the heat, cover with a lid and leave to sit for 4 minutes. Transfer the eggs to a bowl of iced water and allow to cool for a minute or so.

2 While the egg is cooking mash the avocado, lemon juice and some salt and pepper in a small bowl with the back of a fork until completely smooth.

3 Toast the slice of sourdough bread and when it's golden, spread generously with the avocado smush. Peel the egg, slice in two and place the halves on top. Arrange the smoked salmon slices around the egg and sprinkle with chives. Devour.

RESTORATIVE MEALS

Thai Chicken Dumpling Soup

———

Hot and Sour Soup

———

Tomato and Rice Seafood Soup

———

Miso Rice Soup

———

Indian Lentil Bowl

———

Roast Vegetable Chermoula Salad

———

Orange, Feta, Coriander and Barley Salad

———

Sticky Roast Aubergine with Rice Salad

———

Turmeric Sunshine Coconut Stew

———

Courgetti and Beetballs

———

Thai Green Veggie Curry

———

Roast Squash and Crunchy Chickpea Stew

———

Lentil-Loaded Baked Sweet Potato

———

In the introduction to this section I have already mentioned the need for balance – both in life and in food – and the recipes in this chapter serve as a remedy to overindulgence, inconsistency and a whole host of other terrible eating habits. Not that there's anything wrong with a little frivolous indulgence from time to time, but it's essential to have a clutch of recipes you can turn to when you're in need of some serious sustenance: think of a warming bowl of goodness that heats you from the inside out and makes you smile and sigh, safe in the knowledge that you are not only nourishing your body but also your soul. This may feel like a tall order when you're under pressure to put something on the table for dinner but these recipes will help you achieve that; they are not just solo doses of goodness but also delicious feasts for the family. Instant chin ticklers like chicken dumpling soup, hijacked by the fragrant ingredients of a Thai street food market, or a beaming turmeric sunshine coconut stew with tender pieces of sweet potato, are quite simply all you require on the darkest of days.

It's not all steamy bowls of goodness, however; bulky grain salads and roast vegetables also feature when it comes to providing sustenance and substance. Dark and delicious Sticky Roast Aubergine slippers served with herb-spiked rice salad or a fresh and vibrant pearl barley salad with juicy orange segments, feta and coriander are perfect examples of making the most of simple ingredients. Recipes like these are intended to give solace beyond tea and sympathy – sometimes what you really need is some proper nourishment!

Easy comfort food can be tricky to come by but there is something about chicken soup that instantly speaks to me on darker days. With inspiration from vibrant Thai flavours and ingredients, this chicken dumpling soup is made in minutes. The only prerequisite is that you do need good-quality chicken stock, homemade is best but you can now buy fairly decent quality stuff in plastic pouches from most supermarkets, which will also do the trick here.

Hands-on time: 20 minutes | Total time: 25 minutes

THAI CHICKEN DUMPLING SOUP

SERVES 4

1.5 litres good-quality chicken stock

3 carrots, cut into julienne strips

Thumb-sized piece of fresh ginger, very finely chopped

1 long red chilli, thinly sliced on the diagonal

2 tbsp fish sauce

Juice of 1 lime

Large handful of coriander leaves, roughly chopped (reserve the stalks for the dumplings)

Sea salt and freshly ground black pepper

FOR THE CHICKEN DUMPLINGS

2 garlic cloves

1 red chilli

Handful of coriander stalks

200g chicken breasts, roughly chopped

1 tbsp fish sauce

1 large free-range egg, beaten

5 tbsp rice flour

1 First make the dumplings. Put the garlic, chilli and coriander stalks in a food processor and blitz until finely chopped. Add the chicken, fish sauce, beaten egg and 3 tablespoons of the rice flour and blitz again until smooth.

2 Sprinkle a plate evenly with the remaining rice flour and drop tablespoon amounts of the chicken mixture into the flour and roll into little dumplings – you should make 16 balls. Set aside.

3 Bring the chicken stock to the boil in a large pan and add the carrot, ginger and chilli; simmer gently for 4–5 minutes or until the carrot is tender. Reduce the heat and then carefully drop the dumplings into the simmering liquid and cook for 3 minutes or until the dumplings are firm and cooked all the way through (they will rise to the surface once cooked).

4 Stir through the fish sauce, lime juice and coriander leaves. Taste and adjust the broth for seasoning. Serve in deep bowls with a little extra coriander to garnish.

You might think that as I grew up in Ireland hot and sour soup wouldn't necessarily be on my radar, but I have been drawn to these Asian flavours for as long as I have been cooking in the kitchen. A welcome break from the norm, I loved experimenting with recipes found in Asian cookery books and this soup became a regular. The altogether exotic taste combination of spicy, sweet, sour and salty is the main feature of this simple soup and delivers a rewarding clear broth, interrupted only by floating silky strands of cooked egg.

Hands-on time: 15 minutes | Total time: 40 minutes

HOT <u>AND</u> SOUR SOUP

SERVES 4

1.25 litres homemade chicken stock

3 lemongrass stalks, smashed with the back of a knife

Large thumb-sized piece of fresh ginger, thinly sliced

Pared rind and juice of 2 limes

2 red chillies, thinly sliced

6 spring onions, thinly sliced

1 tbsp brown sugar

1 small pumpkin, peeled and cut into cubes

125g oyster mushrooms, ends trimmed

1 tbsp fish sauce

1 large free-range egg, beaten

Large handful of fresh coriander, Thai basil and mint, leaves torn

1 Place the chicken stock, lemongrass, ginger, lime rind, half the chillies and spring onions, and the brown sugar in a large pan. Bring to a steady simmer and cook for 10 minutes until the broth is infused with the aromatic flavours. Strain the soup, discarding the ingredients.

2 Return the broth to the pan and bring back to a steady simmer. Add the pumpkin and simmer for 10 minutes or until the flesh is just tender. Add the mushrooms, lime juice and fish sauce and cook for another 5 minutes, until the mushrooms are tender.

3 Gently swirl the soup with a wooden spoon and slowly trickle the beaten egg into the soup to form thin, silky ribbons.

4 Serve the soup topped with the fresh herbs and remaining chilli and spring onions.

Growing up in a fishing village in Ireland it's hard not to love creamy seafood chowder, with its perfect mix of smoky fish, white fish and a clatter of mussels. When I want all the comfort and heart of a chowder but without the calories, this lighter seafood stew hits the spot.

Hands-on time: 30 minutes | Total time: 45 minutes

TOMATO AND RICE SEAFOOD SOUP

SERVES 4

1 tbsp olive oil

1 onion, finely chopped

1 carrot, finely chopped

1 celery stick, finely chopped

3 garlic cloves, finely chopped

1 red chilli, finely chopped

1 heaped tsp smoked paprika

150g basmati rice

75ml dry white wine

500ml fish stock

2 x 400g tins chopped tomatoes

250g cod fillet, skinned and sliced into 4cm cubes

20 large raw prawns, peeled

500g mussels, cleaned and debearded

Large handful of flat-leaf parsley, roughly chopped

Sea salt and freshly ground black pepper

1 Place a large pan over a medium heat and add the oil. Add the onion, carrot, celery, garlic and chilli and fry for 6–8 minutes until just softened. Season the vegetables with salt and pepper and stir through the paprika and rice, turning to coat in the oil.

2 Add the white wine and allow to simmer for 2 minutes before pouring in the fish stock and chopped tomatoes. Bring the pan to a steady simmer and cook for 10 minutes or until the rice is just al dente.

3 Add the cod, prawns and mussels, cover with a lid and cook for 5 minutes or until the mussels have opened (discard any that remain closed).

4 Serve generous ladles of the stew in deep bowls and sprinkle with the chopped fresh parsley to serve.

There is something instantly restorative about a broth like this. Even the worst head cold would find it hard to withstand its soothing elements. Miso is a fermented paste most commonly made from soy beans and adds an essential salty umami taste to this soup.

Hands-on time: 10 minutes | Total time: 15 minutes

MISO RICE SOUP

SERVES 4

1 tbsp sunflower oil

6 spring onions, thinly sliced

1 red chilli, thinly sliced

Thumb-sized piece of fresh ginger, finely grated

1.5 litres vegetable stock

2 tsp sesame oil

1 tsp light soy sauce

1 tbsp rice wine vinegar

1 tbsp miso paste

125g shitake mushrooms, thinly sliced

75g brown rice, cooked

2 baby bok choy, quartered

1 Place a large pan over a medium heat and add the oil. Add the spring onions, chilli and ginger and fry for 3–4 minutes.

2 Pour in the vegetable stock, sesame oil, soy sauce and rice wine vinegar and then mix in the miso paste.

3 Bring to a steady simmer and then add the mushrooms, cooked brown rice and bok choy. Cook for 5 minutes until the bok choy is tender. Serve immediately.

Indian dahl is a soothing, spiced lentil stew cooked until the pulses have softened to the point of a substantial red mush. I love the spices used and, moreover, it's wonderfully substantial as a supper. Added to this cauliflower and carrot salad it makes a delicious and healthy meal.

Hands-on time: 20 minutes | Total time: 45 minutes

INDIAN LENTIL BOWL

SERVES 4

1 head of cauliflower, cut into florets

1 x 400g tin chickpeas, rinsed and drained

1 tbsp sunflower oil

2 tsp ground cumin

3 carrots, cut into julienne strips

Juice of ½ lemon

Small handful of fresh mint, finely chopped

4 tbsp sunflower seeds, toasted

Sea salt and freshly ground black pepper

FOR THE DAHL

300g red lentils

1 tsp grated fresh ginger

1 tsp ground turmeric

½ tsp ground cumin

Handful of fresh coriander, stalks finely chopped and leaves roughly chopped

1 tsp salt

1 x 400ml tin coconut milk

1 x 400g tin chopped tomatoes

100g baby spinach leaves

1 Preheat the oven to 200°C (180°C fan).

2 Place the cauliflower and chickpeas on a large flat baking tray and drizzle with the oil. Sprinkle with cumin and season with salt and pepper. Toss to combine. Roast in the oven for 25 minutes, then remove and allow to cool.

3 Meanwhile make the dahl. Put the lentils into a medium heavy-based pan with the ginger, turmeric, cumin, coriander stalks and salt, then pour over the coconut milk and 500ml water. Bring to a gentle simmer and cook for 30 minutes, stirring frequently, adding the chopped tomatoes after 10 minutes.

4 Place the carrots in a mixing bowl with the lemon juice and mint leaves and then mix through the cooled roasted cauliflower and chickpeas and sunflower seeds.

5 Stir the baby spinach leaves into the dahl and allow to wilt down. Ladle into bowls, add the roasted cauliflower salad and serve sprinkled with the coriander leaves.

How many ways can you serve roast vegetables? In my case as many ways as I possibly can! Chermoula is a North African marinade that adds subtle yet gutsy spice to these simple roast vegetables. See the vegetables suggested here as merely a suggestion; you can make this salad work with many others you might discover in the bottom of your fridge.

Hands-on time: 15 minutes | Total time: 55–60 minutes

ROAST VEGETABLE CHERMOULA SALAD

SERVES 4

2 red onions, quartered

250g cherry tomatoes, sliced in half

1 x 400g tin chickpeas, rinsed and drained

4 small carrots, peeled and halved lengthways

4 small beetroot, peeled and quartered

6 baby potatoes, sliced in half

150g bulgur wheat, cooked

Sea salt and freshly ground black pepper

FOR THE CHERMOULA

100ml extra-virgin olive oil

Zest and juice of 1 lemon

1½ tsp ground cumin

1 tsp ground coriander

1 tsp smoked paprika

1 tsp cayenne pepper

3 garlic cloves

Large handful of fresh coriander, roughly chopped

Large handful of flat-leaf parsley, roughly chopped

Sea salt and freshly ground black pepper

1 Preheat the oven to 200°C (180°C fan).

2 Blitz all the ingredients for the chermoula in a food processer until smooth. Season to taste.

3 Place the onions, tomatoes, chickpeas, carrots, beetroot and potatoes on a large flat baking tray. Take care not to overcrowd the tray – spread over two baking trays if necessary. Toss the vegetables with 4 tablespoons of the chermoula until completely coated and then season with salt and pepper. Roast in the oven for 40–45 minutes or until all the vegetables are tender.

4 Toss the remaining chermoula through the bulgur wheat, keeping a little back to drizzle over before serving.

5 Serve the roasted vegetables with the bulgur wheat on a large serving platter, drizzled with the last of the chermoula.

Segmenting an orange is a fiddly job but it's one of those kitchen chores – along with peeling Brussels sprouts and podding broad beans – that I find enjoyment in. It's a job worthwhile for a fresh and somewhat alternative salad like this. Don't skimp on the feta here, the contrast between the sweet acidity of the orange with the salty feta is brilliant.

Hands-on time: 10 minutes | Total time: 1 hour

ORANGE, FETA, CORIANDER AND BARLEY SALAD

SERVES 4

250g pearl barley

1 pomegranate

3–4 large oranges, segmented

1 large red onion, thinly sliced

200g feta cheese, crumbled into chunks

Large handful of fresh mint, roughly chopped

Large handful of fresh coriander, roughly chopped

FOR THE DRESSING

6 tbsp extra-virgin olive oil

Zest and juice of 1 lemon

2 garlic cloves, finely grated

2 tbsp pomegranate molasses

Sea salt and freshly ground black pepper

1 Place the pearl barley in a pan and cover with water. Place over a medium-high heat and bring to the boil. Reduce the heat and simmer for 50 minutes, or until the grains are tender and all the cooking liquid has been absorbed. Set aside to cool.

2 Meanwhile mix all the ingredients for the dressing together in a jam jar with a tight-fitting lid and give it a good shake to combine.

3 Cut the pomegranate in half and, holding one half cut side down over a bowl, bash with the back of a wooden spoon to release the seeds. Repeat with the other half.

4 Use a sharp knife to cut away the peel and white pith from the oranges. Cut the oranges into segments, holding them over a large bowl to catch the juices. Drop the segments into the bowl.

5 Add the red onion, crumbled feta, pomegranate seeds, cooked pearl barley and herbs. Pour over the dressing and toss gently to combine. Serve at room temperature.

There is ultimate satisfaction in transforming spongy, purple-fleshed aubergines into something dark, sticky and spiced. They go wonderfully with a meat stew or, as here, with a light rice salad spiked with pomegranate seeds and freshly chopped herbs.

Hands-on time: 10 minutes | **Total time: 35 minutes**

STICKY ROAST AUBERGINE
WITH RICE SALAD

SERVES 4

4 aubergines, sliced in half lengthways

3 tbsp olive oil

3 tbsp ras el hanout

4 tbsp pomegranate molasses

Sea salt and freshly ground black pepper

4 tbsp yoghurt, to serve

FOR THE RICE SALAD

1 large pomegranate

250g basmati rice, cooked and cooled

1 tsp ras el hanout

Juice of 1 lemon

1 x 400g tin chickpeas, rinsed and drained

6 spring onions, thinly sliced

Large handful of fresh mint, parsley and coriander, roughly chopped

Sea salt and freshly ground black pepper

1 Preheat the oven to 200°C (180°C fan).

2 Score the cut sides of the aubergines with a sharp knife to create a diamond pattern. Drizzle generously with olive oil and rub with the ras el hanout until completely coated. Place on a baking tray and roast in the oven for 30 minutes or until the flesh is just tender but still holds its shape. Remove from the oven and brush generously with the pomegranate molasses on all sides. Return to the oven for 5 minutes until caramelised and sticky.

3 For the rice salad, cut the pomegranate in half and, holding one half cut side down over a bowl, bash with the back of a wooden spoon to release the seeds. Repeat with the other half. Add to a bowl with the cooled rice and mix together all the remaining ingredients and season to taste with salt and pepper.

4 Arrange the rice salad and sticky roast aubergine on a large platter and serve with dollops of natural yoghurt.

For those days when only a big, smug bowl of virtuous sunshine will do, this recipe has got you covered! Adapt it with other vegetables as you see fit – butternut squash, pumpkin or a waxy potato will all add substance.

Hands-on time: 15 minutes | Total time: 30 minutes

TURMERIC SUNSHINE COCONUT STEW

SERVES 4

2 tbsp olive oil

1 large onion, finely chopped

3 garlic cloves, finely chopped

1 red chilli, finely chopped

1 tsp ground turmeric (or a thumb-sized piece of fresh turmeric, finely chopped)

1 tbsp curry powder

2 large sweet potatoes, diced

400ml vegetable stock

1 x 400ml tin coconut milk

1 x 400g tin chickpeas, rinsed and drained

Juice of ½ lime

Large handful of fresh coriander, roughly chopped

Sea salt and freshly ground black pepper

1 Place a large pan over a medium heat and add the oil. Add the onion, season with salt and pepper and fry for 6–8 minutes until tender.

2 Add the garlic, chilli, turmeric and curry powder and fry for a further 2 minutes until the spices release their aroma.

3 Add the sweet potato chunks and stir until coated in the spices, then pour in the vegetable stock, coconut milk and chickpeas. Bring back to a steady simmer and cook for 15 minutes or until the sweet potato is just tender.

4 Check the seasoning and stir through the lime juice and coriander. Serve in deep bowls.

While the pun alone is quite satisfying, this very cool take on an Italian classic is completely vegetarian and makes for a simple and light supper. The mixture can also be formed into larger patties to make vegetarian burgers.

Hands-on time: 25–30 minutes | Total time: 30 minutes

COURGETTI AND BEETBALLS

SERVES 4

1 tbsp olive oil

2 garlic cloves, very finely chopped

1 tsp dried chilli flakes

1 x 680g jar passata

3 large, thick courgettes, trimmed

Large handful of fresh basil, leaves torn, plus extra to serve

Sea salt and freshly ground black pepper

Parmesan shavings, to serve

FOR THE BEETBALLS

1 small onion, grated

2 raw beetroot, peeled and grated

2 large carrots, peeled and grated

150g porridge oats

1 x 400g tin chickpeas, rinsed and drained

3 tbsp tahini

Sea salt and freshly ground black pepper

2 tbsp olive oil, for frying

1 First make the beetballs. Using your hands, squeeze all the excess liquid from the grated vegetables (you can do this by wrapping in a clean tea towel, if you prefer). Add to a food processor with the oats, chickpeas and tahini and season with salt and pepper. Blitz until you have a chunky mixture, then form the mixture into 16 bite-sized balls and set aside.

2 To make the sauce heat the oil in a large pan over a medium-high heat. Add the garlic and chilli flakes and fry for 30 seconds before adding the passata. Reduce the heat and allow to simmer for 10 minutes until slightly reduced. Season to taste with salt and pepper.

3 While the sauce is simmering, heat the oil in a large frying pan over a low-medium heat and add the beetballs. Fry for 8–10 minutes or until golden brown on all sides and cooked through.

4 Use a spiraliser to create long noodles from the courgettes (if you don't have a spiraliser you can use a julienne peeler). When the sauce is ready, add the courgettes and basil and toss through to coat the noodles with the sauce.

5 Serve the courgetti in deep plates, topped with the beetballs. Scatter over the Parmesan shavings and remaining basil leaves to serve.

My first taste of an authentic Thai green curry was in Bangkok and was a world apart from the sweet and creamy, subtly spiced variation we are used to in the Western world. Using a traditional recipe from the kitchens of Thai royalty, the curry was creamy but instead of being spicy, it had an almost overwhelming taste of aniseed coming from the Thai holy basil leaves. This basil is completely different from its Italian cousin, and well worth tracking down to complete this simple curry. Realistically, most home cooks won't have access to all the ingredients required for the fully authentic version, so this is a slightly simplified variation that peps up store-bought curry paste to give you very decent results. Find the best Thai green curry paste and Thai holy basil in Asian food stores.

Hands-on time: 20 minutes | Total time: 20 minutes

THAI GREEN VEGGIE CURRY

SERVES 4

1 thumb-sized piece of fresh ginger, finely grated

2 lemongrass stalks, very finely chopped

3 garlic cloves, finely chopped

Zest and juice of 1 lime

2 handfuls of Thai basil leaves, torn, plus extra to garnish

4 tbsp Thai green curry paste

1 x 400ml tin coconut milk

250ml vegetable stock

1 tbsp light brown sugar

2 tbsp fish sauce

2 baby bok choy, sliced into quarters

150g sugar snap peas

100g beansprouts, plus extra to garnish

250g brown basmati rice, cooked

Chopped red chilli, to garnish (optional)

1 Place the ginger, lemongrass, garlic, lime zest and half the Thai basil in a pestle and mortar and bash until smooth. Add the curry paste and mix through.

2 Pour the coconut milk into a wok or large pan and bring to a steady simmer. Add the pepped-up curry paste and stir continuously until the paste is incorporated into the coconut milk.

3 Pour in the vegetable stock, sugar and fish sauce and bring back to simmering point. Allow to simmer for 2 minutes until slightly reduced.

4 Add in the bok choy, sugar snap peas and beansprouts and cook for 3–5 minutes until the vegetables are tender. Stir through the remaining Thai basil until just wilted.

5 Serve the curry with rice and scatter with a few Thai basil leaves and beansprouts. If you want an extra hit of heat, add a little chopped chilli before serving.

This simple stew is a cinch to prepare but delivers layers of deep spice. Ras el hanout is a blend of spices used mainly in North African cuisine and can typically contain more than 20 spices, including dried peppers, cardamom, nutmeg, cinnamon, cloves, allspice and fennel. Look for it in Asian or Middle Eastern stores – if you can't get hold of it you could replace with another spice blend like garam masala.

Hands-on time: 20 minutes | **Total time: 45–50 minutes**

ROAST SQUASH AND CRUNCHY CHICKPEA STEW

SERVES 4

1 large butternut squash, peeled and cut into small cubes

1–2 tbsp olive oil

2 tbsp ras el hanout

1 x 400g tin chickpeas, rinsed and drained

1 large onion, finely chopped

3 carrots, finely chopped

3 garlic cloves, finely chopped

500ml vegetable stock

1 x 400g tin chopped tomatoes

1 heaped tbsp harissa paste

150g baby spinach leaves

Large handful of flat-leaf parsley, roughly chopped

Sea salt and freshly ground black pepper

1 Preheat the oven to 220°C (200°C fan).

2 Tip the butternut squash onto a large, flat baking tray and drizzle with olive oil and a tablespoon of the ras el hanout. Do the same with the chickpeas on a separate baking tray. Season both with salt and pepper and place in the oven. Roast the chickpeas for 20–25 minutes or until golden and crisp and the butternut squash for 35–40 minutes or until tender and slightly charred at the edges.

3 Meanwhile place a large pan over a medium heat and add a generous glug of oil. Fry the onion, carrots and garlic for 6–8 minutes or until softened. Season with salt and pepper.

4 Add the vegetable stock, chopped tomatoes and harissa paste. Bring to a steady simmer and cook for 15 minutes. Add the roasted squash and spinach and stir through for 1 minute or until the spinach has wilted. Stir through half the parsley and season to taste.

5 Serve in deep bowls and top with the remaining chopped parsley and the crispy roast chickpeas.

There is something comforting about the mushy sweetness of a baked sweet potato. It is the perfect vehicle for lots of different fillings, but for a proper supper that will fill you up, pile them high with curried lentils and perhaps a dollop of yoghurt.

Hands-on time: 20 minutes | **Total time: 1 hour 20 minutes**

LENTIL-LOADED BAKED SWEET POTATO

SERVES 4

4 small sweet potatoes

100g grated mature Cheddar cheese, plus extra to top

FOR THE LENTILS

1 tbsp rapeseed oil

1 large onion, finely chopped

3 garlic cloves, finely chopped

2 tbsp ground cumin

1 tbsp ground coriander

1 tsp chilli powder

1 tsp smoked paprika

250g Puy lentils

2 x 400g tins plum tomatoes

1.25 litres vegetable stock

1 x 400g tin kidney beans, rinsed and drained

Sea salt and freshly ground black pepper

1 First prepare the lentils. Heat the oil in a large casserole over a medium-high heat. Add the onion and fry for 4–5 minutes until just tender. Stir in the garlic, cumin, coriander, chilli powder and paprika and fry for a further 2–3 minutes. Preheat the oven to 200°C (180°C fan).

2 Add the lentils, plum tomatoes and vegetable stock to the casserole and bring to the boil. Reduce the heat slightly, season with salt and pepper and simmer gently for 45 minutes or until the lentils are tender and cooked through.

3 Place the sweet potatoes on a baking tray and bake for 40 minutes or until tender when pierced with a fork.

4 Add the kidney beans to the casserole and cook for a further 5 minutes. Taste and adjust the seasoning.

5 When the sweet potatoes are cooked, split in half lengthways with a sharp knife. Scoop out a little of the sweet potato to make a well in the centre and add to the lentils along with the grated cheese. Divide the mixture between each sweet potato half, sprinkle with a little extra grated cheese and place back in the oven for 15–20 minutes. Serve with some mixed salad leaves.

SIMPLE SUPPERS, SALADS AND SNACKS

———

Green Pumped Quesadillas

———

Cabbage Rolls with Nutty Dipping Sauce

———

Pea and Feta Salad

———

Shredded Brussels Sprout Salad

———

No-cook Nutty Noodle Jar Salad

———

Sweet Potato Tortilla with Caramelised Onions

———

Quinoa Halloumi Cakes

———

Spelt Spaghetti and Avocado Pesto

———

Miso Salmon and Smacked Cucumber Salad

———

Blitzed Oat Baked Cod

———

Brussels Sprout Chips

———

Harissa Nut Mix

———

Superfood Popcorn

———

Peanut Butter Cups

———

Good food on the go can be tough to get right; walk into any convenience store and all those terrible options will be practically jumping off the shelves at you, especially when you're hungry. I'm pretty sure that plastic-wrapped sandwiches from the chiller cabinet are not what the majority of us want to eat when it comes to lunchtime.

Sure, nowadays there are plenty of better options out there for you, but then how would you get that smug satisfaction from knowing that you have the best lunch in the whole office and that you made it yourself? In my book there's no getting away from the fact that a homemade lunch is always the better option. Yes, it does require a bit of preparation and planning but taking time the night before to think through your lunch options makes for better food choices in the long run. You'll be the envy of the workplace with colourful Cabbage Rolls with Nutty Dipping Sauce or No-cook Nutty Noodle Jar Salad in a creamy satay sauce, while snacks like the Harissa Nut Mix, Superfood Popcorn or Brussels Sprout Chips are bound to raise a few eyebrows.

Hopefully these recipes will help inspire you to create your own great food on the go.

I make no excuses for loving the simplicity of piling ingredients into tortilla wraps, sandwiching them together with cheese and toasting until meltingly delicious. My go-to version includes just cheese, red onion and salsa so this slightly healthier version is my compromise. Oozing with all the same flavour, it's pumped with spinach, avocado and black beans to make a more substantial quick supper fix. And for anyone like me who ends up buying those teeny jars of salsa that leave you wanting more, I hope you'll be thoroughly satisfied with this quick blitz salsa, which makes enough to have as a fresh and spicy dipping sauce alongside your glorified 'healthy' cheese toasty!

Hands-on time: 15 minutes | Total time: 25 minutes

GREEN PUMPED QUESADILLAS

SERVES 4

8 wholewheat tortilla wraps

1 large red onion, thinly sliced

1 x 400g tin black beans, rinsed and drained

2 large ripe avocados, thinly sliced

150g baby spinach leaves, roughly chopped

200g Cheddar cheese, grated

4 tsp oil

FOR THE SALSA

1 x 400g tin whole peeled cherry tomatoes

1 small onion, roughly chopped

1 green chilli, roughly chopped

2 garlic cloves, roughly chopped

Large handful of fresh coriander

Juice of 1 lime

Sea salt and freshly ground black pepper

1 Whizz all the ingredients for the salsa in a small food processor until smooth; taste and adjust the seasoning.

2 Spread 2 tablespoons of the salsa on one of the wholewheat wraps. Top with a quarter of the red onion, black beans, avocado slices and chopped spinach. Sprinkle over a quarter of the grated cheese and press tightly with another tortilla wrap.

3 Heat a teaspoon of the oil in a frying pan over a low heat and add the quesadilla to the pan. Fry for 2–3 minutes on each side or until golden brown and the cheese has melted. Carefully transfer to a chopping board and then slice into quarters.

4 Repeat with the remaining wraps and serve warm with a small dipping bowl of the remaining salsa.

In the case of most TV crew lunches you're doing pretty well if you get a fancy sandwich but I was recently filming in Los Angeles, where they know how to do lunch right! Alongside clever salads and lighter sandwiches there were these cabbage rolls. Stick with me, they are a truly Californian invention, sturdy enough to withstand the confines of a lunchbox while also being nutritious and, dare I say, delicious too! In the States they use large, leafy collard greens (a member of the brassica family) but curly-leaved savoy cabbage will do the job. Blanching makes slightly thicker leaves more pliable but you won't need to do this if your leaves are already quite thin.

Hands-on time: 20 minutes | Total time: 20 minutes

CABBAGE ROLLS WITH NUTTY DIPPING SAUCE

SERVES 4

12 medium savoy cabbage leaves, tough stalks removed

200g hummus (shop-bought or homemade, see page 38)

75g quinoa, cooked

¼ small red cabbage (about 200g), thinly sliced

1 large carrot (about 175g), cut into julienne strips

4 spring onions, cut lengthways into thin julienne strips

FOR THE DIPPING SAUCE

4 tbsp smooth peanut butter

Juice of 1 lime

2 tsp sriracha sauce

1 tbsp honey

2 tbsp dark soy sauce

1 Bring a large, wide pan of water to the boil. Add the cabbage leaves and blanch for 2 minutes. Drain and refresh under cold water and then pat dry with kitchen paper. Set aside.

2 In a small bowl, mix together all the ingredients for the dipping sauce, loosening with about 4 tablespoons of water.

3 Assemble the rolls by placing a cabbage leaf on a chopping board. Spread generously with hummus before adding a few tablespoons of quinoa. Carefully add strips of red cabbage, carrot and spring onion and then roll up tightly.

4 Repeat with the remaining cabbage leaves and filling and then serve the rolls with the nutty dipping sauce.

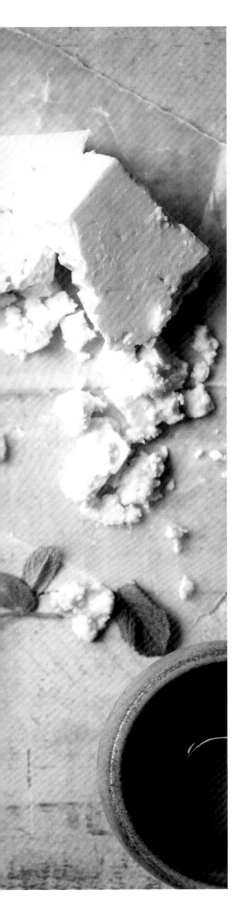

This simple side dish of sweet peas, tossed with salty, crumbly feta with a sharp lemon vinaigrette goes perfectly with grilled meats during the summer. Made with just frozen peas this salad is delicious but I love the textural addition of sugar snap peas here, and if you can get your hands on pea shoots bung them in – they will make all the difference to the presentation.

Hands-on time: 5 minutes | Total time: 10 minutes

PEA AND FETA SALAD

SERVES 4–6

250g frozen peas

250g sugar snap peas

200g feta cheese, crumbled

Large handful of fresh mint leaves, roughly torn

Pea shoots, to garnish

FOR THE DRESSING

2 tbsp extra-virgin olive oil

Squeeze of lemon juice

1 tsp white wine vinegar

1 garlic clove, finely grated

1 tsp honey

Sea salt and freshly ground black pepper

1 Whisk together all the ingredients for the dressing until completely combined; taste and adjust the seasoning.

2 Cook the frozen peas and sugar snap peas in a large pan of salted boiling salted water for 4–5 minutes. Drain and rinse under cold water to cool completely, then allow to drain thoroughly.

3 Place the peas, feta and mint in a large serving bowl. Add the dressing and toss to combine, then garnish with the pea shoots. Serve straight away.

When we have friends round for dinner I am a big believer that most of the work in the kitchen should be done before they arrive – that way I can actually enjoy myself once they're here. Salads like this are the way forward. This one can be made up to a day in advance and will sit quite happy in the fridge until you are ready to serve. Using a food processor with the blade attachment will make short work of shredding the Brussels – broccoli and fennel also work well here.

Hands-on time: 10 minutes | Total time: 10 minutes

SHREDDED BRUSSELS SPROUT SALAD

Marino Branch
Brainse Marglann Mhuirín
Tel: 8336297

SERVES 4

1 large pomegranate

500g Brussels sprouts, roots and outer leaves trimmed

75g skinless roasted hazelnuts, chopped

50g pecorino cheese, shaved (optional)

FOR THE DRESSING

2 tbsp white wine vinegar

2 tsp Dijon mustard

6 tbsp extra-virgin olive oil

2 garlic cloves, very finely chopped

2 tsp honey

Sea salt and freshly ground black pepper

1 Whisk together all the ingredients for the dressing until completely combined.

2 Cut the pomegranate in half and, holding one half cut side down over a bowl, bash with the back of a wooden spoon to release the seeds. Repeat with the other half.

3 Using a food processor with a fine blade attachment, shave the Brussels sprouts finely. Add to a large mixing bowl with the pomegranate seeds, half the hazelnuts and half the pecorino.

4 Add the dressing and toss gently to combine. Turn out onto a serving platter and sprinkle over the remaining nuts and pecorino cheese before serving.

There is something wonderfully satisfying about the slipperiness of this nutty, Asian-inspired noodle salad. The true beauty of it however is the ease in which can be assembled – whisking, shredding and spiralising your way to simple lunchbox smugness!

Hands-on time: 15 minutes | Total time: 15 minutes

NO-COOK NUTTY NOODLE JAR SALAD

SERVES 2

2 large fat courgettes, trimmed

2 carrots, peeled with a julienne peeler

1 cucumber, peeled with a julienne peeler

½ head of Chinese cabbage, shredded

4 spring onions, thinly sliced

1 avocado, thinly sliced

3 tbsp sesame seeds, toasted

Large handful of fresh coriander leaves, roughly chopped

50g mixed sprouted seeds, such as alfafa, lentil, radish, broccoli

FOR THE PEANUT SAUCE

150g peanut butter, preferably crunchy

6 tbsp tamari

2 tbsp rice wine vinegar

1 tbsp honey

1 tbsp sriracha sauce

2 garlic cloves, very finely chopped

Thumb-sized piece of fresh ginger, very finely chopped

1 In a large mixing bowl, whisk together all the ingredients for the peanut sauce until completely combined.

2 Spiralise the courgettes so you are left with a tangle of vegetable noodles. Add these to the mixing bowl.

3 Add the carrots, cucumber, Chinese cabbage, spring onions, avocado, 2 tablespoons of the sesame seeds and most of the the coriander leaves. Toss everything together to coat.

4 Transfer to jars or lunchboxes and top with the sprouts, remaining sesame seeds and coriander.

I've always viewed a Spanish tortilla as more of an in-between dinner, certainly not a showstopper of a dinner, but a simple dish that is good for making use of leftover meat and vegetables. This variation may just put a stop to that! Plump and pudgy with tender sweet potatoes, smoky roast red peppers and caramelised red onions, there is more than a slight air of smug sophistication with this fancy version! Any leftovers are delicious enjoyed warm the next day.

Hands-on time: 30 minutes | Total time: 50–55 minutes

SWEET POTATO TORTILLA
WITH CARAMELISED ONIONS

SERVES 4

2 tbsp olive oil

2 red onions, thinly sliced

3 garlic cloves, very finely chopped

Few thyme sprigs, leaves picked

1 large sweet potato, peeled and cut into thin half moons

100g baby spinach leaves

6 large free-range eggs

90g roasted red peppers from a jar, sliced

Sea salt and freshly ground black pepper

100g rocket leaves, to serve

Extra-virgin olive oil and lemon juice, to serve

1 Heat a large, ovenproof frying pan over a low-medium heat and add a tablespoon of the olive oil. Add the onions, season with salt and pepper and fry gently for 8 minutes or until softened. Stir through the garlic and thyme and cook for a further 2 minutes.

2 Add the sweet potato slices and 3 tablespoons of cold water, cover with a lid and cook for 15 minutes until just tender, stirring occasionally. Just before the sweet potato is cooked, stir through the spinach until just wilted.

3 In a bowl, whisk together the eggs until just beaten. Season with salt and pepper and add the contents of the pan to the bowl along with the roasted red peppers. Mix until completely incorporated.

4 Add the remaining oil to the pan and place back on the heat. Tip the contents of the bowl back into the pan and cook until the bottom is just set. Place the pan under a moderate grill for 10–15 minutes, until the tortilla is puffed up and golden brown on top.

5 Serve generous slices of the tortilla with the rocket leaves, drizzled with extra-virgin olive oil and a squeeze of lemon juice.

I do love a good recipe that makes use of the leftovers sitting in my fridge. These quinoa cakes, spiked with salty halloumi cheese and spiced with paprika and cayenne pepper, are a perfect example – serve them with a dressed salad for a light lunch. The uncooked cakes can be kept in the fridge for up to 5 days and also freeze well, should you want to prepare some in advance.

Hands-on time: 30 minutes | Total time: 30 minutes

QUINOA HALLOUMI CAKES

SERVES 4

200g cooked quinoa

200g halloumi, coarsely grated

3 tbsp wholemeal flour

1 large free-range egg

1 garlic clove, finely grated

3 spring onions, finely chopped

1 tsp smoked paprika

1 tsp cayenne pepper

Sea salt and freshly ground black pepper

Olive oil, for frying

TO SERVE

6 tbsp natural yoghurt

½ tsp smoked paprika

Dressed salad leaves

1 Place all the ingredients for the cakes in a large bowl and mix well until evenly combined. Divide the mixture into eight and shape into burger patties.

2 Heat a large frying pan over a low-medium heat and add a glug of oil. Fry the cakes in batches for 3–4 minutes on each side until golden brown.

3 Mix together the yoghurt and smoked paprika and season to taste. Serve the cakes with a dollop of the spiced yoghurt and some dressed salad leaves on the side.

This dairy-free pesto gives quick and satisfying results, providing a silky and substantial sauce for pasta. Spelt pasta is often easier to digest than wheat, which is why I've suggested it here – its bite and flavour adds an extra dimension to this simple dish.

Hands-on time: 4 minutes | Total time: 12–14 minutes

SPELT SPAGHETTI AND AVOCADO PESTO

SERVES 4

300g spelt spaghetti or linguine

150g sun-blushed tomatoes, roughly chopped

FOR THE PESTO

1 ripe avocado, peeled and stoned

100g basil leaves and stalks, plus a few leaves to garnish

50g pine nuts

50ml extra-virgin olive oil

2 garlic cloves

Juice of ½ lemon

Sea salt and freshly ground black pepper

1 Bring a large pan of salted water to the boil and cook the pasta until al dente.

2 While the pasta is cooking blitz all the ingredients for the pesto in a food processor until smooth. Taste and adjust the seasoning.

3 Drain the cooked pasta and return it to the pan. Add the pesto and sun-blushed tomatoes. Toss the pasta until completely coated and serve in deep bowls, garnished with a few extra basil leaves.

A tender fillet of warm salmon in a sticky umami glaze is delicious on its own, but combined with brown rice and a smacked cucumber salad you are in for an Asian treat. 'Smacked cucumber salad?!' I hear you cry. Fear not, the salad of softened pieces of cucumber in a sharp pickle with cabbage, beansprouts and toasted sesame seeds will have you converted.

Hands-on time: 10 minutes | **Total time: 35–40 minutes, plus resting and marinating**

MISO SALMON AND SMACKED CUCUMBER SALAD

SERVES 4

4 skinless salmon fillets (about 120g each)

250g brown sticky rice

FOR THE MISO MARINADE

2 tbsp miso paste

1 tbsp rice wine

2 tbsp light soy sauce

2 tsp caster sugar

2 spring onions, very thinly sliced

2 tsp sesame oil

FOR THE SMACKED CUCUMBER SALAD

1 cucumber

50ml rice wine vinegar

3 tbsp caster sugar

½ head of Chinese cabbage, very thinly sliced

200g beansprouts

3 tbsp sesame seeds, toasted

Sea salt and freshly ground black pepper

1 To make the smacked cucumber salad, place the cucumber on a chopping board and smash several times with a rolling pin, then cut in half, scoop out the seeds and cut into thin batons. Place the rice wine vinegar and sugar in a serving bowl and whisk until the sugar has dissolved. Add the cucumber batons, Chinese cabbage and beansprouts and toss to coat. Cover with cling film and set aside for at least 10 minutes, or up to 8 hours in the fridge is fine.

2 Place the salmon in a deep-sided baking dish. Whisk together the ingredients for the miso marinade and pour over the salmon, turning until completely coated. Cover and leave to marinate in the fridge for 30 minutes and up to 2 hours.

3 Preheat the oven to 200°C (180°C fan) and bring a large pan of salted water to the boil. Cook the brown rice for 25–30 minutes or according to the instructions on the packet.

4 While the rice is cooking pour off any excess marinade from the salmon and then arrange the salmon fillets flat side down in the baking dish. Bake in the oven for 15 minutes until the salmon is cooked through and flakes easily with a fork.

5 Serve the salmon fillets with the cooked brown rice and cucumber salad.

Definitely not your traditional fish and chips; this lovely, lighter alternative is a simple supper to prepare. You can make the super green tartare sauce with just parsley but do add the dill and chives to amp up the flavour if you have them. Do make sure you use a large enough tray – the sweet potato chips need to spread out enough to prevent them from sweating and becoming too mushy.

Hands-on time: 10 minutes | Total time: 35 minutes

BLITZED OAT BAKED COD

SERVES 2

1 large sweet potato, sliced into thin chips

1 tbsp rapeseed oil

25g wholewheat flour

1 large free-range egg, beaten

50g oats, whizzed to a rough crumb

2 skinless and boneless cod fillets (about 150g each)

Sea salt and freshly ground black pepper

FOR THE TARTAR SAUCE

3 tbsp Greek yoghurt

1 tsp capers

3 cornichons

Small handful of fresh parsley

Small handful of fresh dill

Small handful of chives

Squeeze of lemon juice

¼ tsp Dijon mustard

Sea salt and freshly ground black pepper

1 Preheat the oven to 200°C (180°C fan).

2 Place the sweet potato chips on a large baking tray, drizzle with the oil and season with salt and pepper. Shake to ensure the chips are evenly coated and then place in the oven to bake for 20 minutes.

3 Place the flour, beaten egg and blitzed oats into three separate bowls. Dredge each cod fillet in flour, dusting off any excess before dipping in egg and then coating in the oat crumbs. Set aside.

4 When the sweet potato chips have had their 20 minutes, remove the tray from the oven and increase the heat to 220°C (200°C fan). Push the chips to the sides to allow room for the cod and then place the coated fish on the tray. Return to the oven for a further 10–12 minutes or until the fish is golden and crisp and the chips are tender and slightly charred on the outside, turning halfway through the cooking time.

5 While the fish is in the oven place all the ingredients for the tartar sauce in a small food processor and blitz until completely smooth. Taste and adjust the seasoning.

6 Serve the fish and chips with a generous dollop of super green tartar sauce.

I know, I know but wait, come back, I haven't turned complete hipster, I promise. In developing any healthy recipe my prerequisite is that it has to deliver serious flavour and that's what these sprout chips do! Brussels sprouts get a bad rep from their traditional role as an over-boiled Christmas side but treated right, like any brassica they can shine. They roast beautifully and become crisp and ideal for virtuous snacking. Nutritional yeast might be a new one to you – it adds savoury texture to these chips and can be found in most health food shops. If you can't find it, however, the recipe will work fine without.

Hands-on time: 20 minutes | Total time: 40 minutes, plus soaking

BRUSSELS SPROUT CHIPS

SERVES 2

100g cashews

500g large Brussels sprouts, roots trimmed and halved

2 tbsp olive oil

1 garlic clove

Juice of ½ lemon

4 tbsp nutritional yeast flakes

Sea salt and freshly ground black pepper

1 Preheat the oven to 200°C (180°C fan).

2 Place the cashews in a small bowl and pour over just enough water to cover them. Soak for at least 2 hours or overnight if possible.

3 Peel away the leaves from the sprouts with your fingers (this is a little fiddly), until you are left with a hefty pile of leaves. Toss the leaves in a bowl with the olive oil and season scantily with salt and pepper.

4 Drain the cashews and then add to a food processor with the garlic, lemon juice and nutritional yeast and blitz with 3 tablespoons of water until smooth. Pour this mixture over the Brussels sprout leaves and toss until everything is evenly combined.

5 Spread over a large flat baking tray, making sure you separate out any that may have clumped together and roast in the oven for 20 minutes until the leaves are crisp and browned, turning halfway through.

6 Enjoy warm from the oven, or re-crisp in the oven again when you are ready to serve.

I often wonder why I don't roast nuts more often for a snack; they are immensely satisfying and I always have some knocking around my cupboards. Here harissa paste and honey add a sticky spiciness that elevates their addictiveness.

Hands-on time: 2 minutes | Total time: 12–14 minutes

HARISSA NUT MIX

SERVES 4

100g almonds

100g walnuts

100g cashew nuts

1 tbsp olive oil

3 tbsp honey

2 tbsp harissa paste

1 tbsp fresh rosemary leaves, finely chopped

Sea salt and freshly ground black pepper

1 Preheat the oven to 180°C (160°C fan).

2 Add all the ingredients to a medium mixing bowl and mix until thoroughly coated.

3 Spread the nuts across a large flat baking tray and then bake in the oven for 10–12 minutes or until toasted and golden. Allow to cool slightly before tucking in!

While wholesome living doesn't always include pigging out with a big bowl of popcorn on the sofa, I feel this popcorn seasoning may just give you the excuse. Turmeric and spirulina have a long list of health benefits and add both colour and flavour to this mix, along with a spicy hit from cayenne pepper and smoked paprika.

Hands-on time: 5 minutes | Total time: 5 minutes

SUPERFOOD POPCORN

SERVES 4

2 tbsp coconut oil

100g popcorn kernels

3 tbsp nutritional yeast flakes

1 tsp ground turmeric

1 tsp spirulina powder

1 tsp smoked paprika

¼ tsp cayenne pepper

2 tsp sea salt

1 Melt the coconut oil in a large, lidded pan over a medium-high heat. Add the popcorn kernels and place the lid on top. Cook until most of the kernels have popped (this should take a couple of minutes).

2 Shake the remaining ingredients together in a small jar and pour over the popcorn in the pan. Replace the lid and shake until everything is coated.

3 Dig in while still warm.

All right, I confess to gorging on those addictive American peanut butter cups every time I visit the States. Chocolate and peanut butter is a combination that works extremely well, a fact that big American candy corporations know all too well! This homemade version will convince you that you never need to buy them again.

Hands-on time: 10 minutes | Total time: 20 minutes

PEANUT BUTTER CUPS

MAKES 10

Cooking spray oil

250g dark chocolate (70% cocoa solids)

2 tbsp coconut oil

200g smooth peanut butter

50g ground almonds

1 Line a cupcake tin with paper cases and spray with oil.

2 Break the dark chocolate into pieces and place in a heatproof bowl with the coconut oil. Set the bowl over a small pan of barely simmering water until melted, making sure the base of the bowl doesn't touch the water.

3 Meanwhile mix the peanut butter and ground almonds together in a bowl until evenly combined.

4 Divide half the melted chocolate between the 10 paper cases and place in the freezer for 10 minutes to set slightly.

5 Remove from the freezer and divide the peanut butter mixture between the paper cases. Now top each one with the remaining chocolate and leave in a cool place to set completely before tucking in. Store in the fridge in an airtight container for up to 1 week.

GO

I think I will always have a love for travel. It's often said that travel becomes a bug: something you catch and you just can't shake off – it becomes addictive to explore the unknown. Of course, travel has its ups and downs but the pleasure in those moments where I find myself in bustling night markets, learning little-known cooking techniques and witnessing the beauty of some of the world's most spectacular landscapes instantly outweigh the rigmarole of packing, airport security, not being able to find that charger that you know you packed and dragging suitcases across hostile terrain.

In the last five years I've visited over 20 countries, both for work and on holiday, and each time I pull out my passport I get that same fuzzy feeling that tells me that good things are coming. My parents always encouraged us to travel; my dad was incapable of sitting still, so our family holidays were more likely to be based around battling the elements on a boat in some isolated waters of the Mediterranean,

rather than sitting by a pool in the sun. When it comes to a sense of adventure the apple doesn't fall far from the tree; while I may not be jumping out of aeroplanes, a journey of discovery will always be more appealing to me than a simple relaxing holiday.

When my wife Sofie and I first started seeing each other in our late teens and early twenties we had the small issue of her living in Sweden and me living in Ireland. With numerous flights back and forth between the two countries we quickly mastered the art of travelling with little money, learning to discover the best of what each country had to offer. Summers spent exploring forests and lakes on the west coast of Sweden and road trips to some of Ireland's most breathtaking spots around the country became part of the process. Pretty soon we were saving up our cash to go further afield, but by then we knew how to make the most of our trips. I will never forget that first nerve-racking visit to Thailand and Vietnam where we had nothing planned and

just hit the ground running. Tweets, emails and Facebook messages to locals brought us closer to the best food and places to visit while frantic map-reading and googling cemented our plans for each day. The excitement of the unknown instantly lit a fire within us and it's why we travel as often as we can, whether for business or pleasure.

As I write this we are in a nomadic state living between Dublin, London, Gothenburg and Los Angeles while we figure out our life plans. This uncertain living situation naturally creates anxiousness on both mine and Sofie's part but we have learned that some of the best things in life come from stepping outside our comfort zone. We also know it's not forever; instead it's a time in our lives we will look back at and remember as a fleeting moment of ambiguity and adventure, a time when we have managed to explore some of the best that these cities have to offer.

When it comes to food and travel, without doubt the best

advice I've ever had (and still follow without fail) is to 'eat where the locals eat'. This single piece of guidance has brought me to some of the most intimidating, remarkable, bizarre and incredible kitchens of the world. For some reason the best food is almost always found down back alleys, at night markets, whether at breakfast or dinner time, sitting elbow to elbow with bemused locals staring at you as you sweat through spicy dishes or guzzle down local delicacies. Does food taste better when you are stepping outside of your comfort zone? I'm inclined to think so. A sense of adventure, nerves of steel and an iron stomach are essential if you are going to sample world cuisines in an authentic way.

While I am slightly averse to the idea of stuffy, organised tourist tours, some of the best food markets I've been to would still be a blur had we not reached out to local tours and guides. I'm not suggesting you sign up to the first bus tour with 30 other tourists, snapping pictures of locals like

a recently descended plague of locusts. Instead spend time to seek out knowledgeable local food lovers who can demystify market ingredients and who will take time to explain how they are used in local cuisines.

While in Vietnam we travelled under the watchful eye of Mr Long, a government official, and local fixer called TT. On the few free evenings we had in Hanoi, TT would stick me on the back of his bike and we'd do a quick-fire tour of his favourite food haunts: snails cooked in a lemongrass broth, spicy beef and papaya salad, thinly sliced pig's ear tossed in a savoury rice powder and rolled up in rice paper with fresh herbs and local beer, with salty and chewy dried squid were all devoured in the space of a couple of hours. Now that's the sort of food travel that gets me excited and the type of eating that would only come with the knowledge of a local.

My favourite travel moments are often the ones that the camera misses. A highlight of my trip around Italy while filming a series called Grandma's Boy was when we found ourselves high in the hills in Montalcino, in the small village of Sant'Angelo in Colle, a haven for Italian nonnas in the know! We learned how to make donzelle, little fried savoury doughnuts, which were delicious with wafer-thin slices of prosciutto and local wine. The most special moment for me

came right before sunset, when I was dragged practically by the ear into a small community kitchen where a group of nattering jolly grannies insisted that I learn how to make a local pasta called pici, a fat, hand-rolled spaghetti. It was just one of those magic moments: I was completely immersed in a local community learning secrets of classic cooking I could only have ever dreamed of. After filming our sunset sequence we sat late into the evening, our table lit by street lamps, laughing and singing obscure Italian songs. The stuff of travel dreams!

Without doubt the countries I have visited over the last five or ten years have influenced and helped form the way I cook today. I travel with a notebook and a camera, two essential tools to capture the brilliant moments and inspirational ideas that I would otherwise forget. This section of the book is a real ode to the recipes, dishes, techniques and characters I've discovered over the last few years, and hopefully gives an insight in to the world of flavours that has been opened up to me. The beautiful thing about travelling the world is that there is no end to it, it's ever-changing – there is always something new to discover. Now... where to next?

FOREIGN
FEASTS

———

Baked Feta Salad

———

Turkish Eggs with Yoghurt

———

Stuffed Peppers

———

Eleni's Filo Pastry Pies

———

Orecchiette with Kale and Pangrattato

———

Middle Eastern Bread Salad

———

Vietnamese Chicken Salad

———

Swedish Chanterelle and Västerbottensost Tart

———

Hungarian Chicken Paprikash with Dumplings

———

Eleni's Giant Bean and Tomato Stew

———

Chicken Zgvacet

———

Butterscotch Pudding with Salted Caramel and Crème Fraîche

———

Rice Pudding with Caramel Topping

———

When I'm travelling I often find myself invited to family gatherings or meals to celebrate special occasions. It's a wonderful thing to be a part of and really gives me an insight into authentic home cooking – something I have always been far more taken with than any sort of restaurant food. A table groaning with platters piled with grilled meats and bowls of interesting salads or dishes of slow-cooked stews and roast vegetables are always far more interesting to me than a single, flawless serving of perfect food.

Most of the foreign feasts I've been lucky enough to attend have one common theme: simple and delicious food that can easily be prepared in advance. From the Italian nonnas to the male chefs of San Sebastian's secret gastronomic societies, the thread that ties them together is recipes that allow the host to make it all look effortless while serving up incredible food.

Many of the recipes in this chapter have been shared with me from the people I have met while traveling and lend themselves extremely well to a celebration spread. Baked feta crumbled through a Greek salad, a big bowl of Middle Eastern Bread Salad or slow-cooked Hungarian spiced chicken stew served straight to the table – all these dishes are simple and clever, the types of dishes I enjoy serving the most.

A Greek salad with a difference. By baking the feta, you not only have an interesting contrast of warm, salty cheese and a crisp, fresh salad, you are also infusing it with the heat of chilli and the aromatic tastes of garlic and oregano. It might sound odd, but a drizzle of sweet and floral honey as you serve the baked feta over the salad, would add something truly special.

Hands-on time: 5 minutes | Total time: 15 minutes

BAKED FETA SALAD

SERVES 2

200g feta cheese

1 small red chilli, finely chopped

1 garlic clove, finely chopped

1 tsp dried oregano

1 tbsp olive oil

FOR THE SALAD

1 cucumber, halved lengthways, seeds scooped out and sliced

250g cherry tomatoes, halved

½ red onion, thinly sliced

200g green and black olives, pitted

1 tbsp red wine vinegar

3 tbsp extra-virgin olive oil

Sea salt and freshly ground black pepper

1 Preheat the oven to 200°C (180°C fan).

2 Place the feta in a small baking tin and sprinkle with the chilli, garlic and oregano. Drizzle with olive oil and bake in the oven for 10 minutes.

3 Place all the ingredients for the salad in a bowl and toss together until well combined. Season the salad with a little salt and pepper.

4 Arrange the salad on a serving platter, arrange the baked feta on top and serve.

Before visiting Istanbul the common piece of advice offered was, 'try the Turkish breakfast!' – solid guidance indeed it turned out to be. One very early morning after the call to prayer had echoed across the city, I sat with our local guide and a camera crew at a table, which began to struggle under the weight of the amount of food being served. Turkish breakfasts are a leisurely affair and are often served throughout the day. They vary but ours consisted of scrambled eggs with sausage, onions and tomatoes, pickled sweet black walnuts in syrup, soft creamy clotted cream with honey and these poached eggs spiced with chilli and paprika, sitting in a well of yoghurt, as well as fresh vegetables, herbs and cheese. A veritable feast! This recipe should help transport you...

Hands-on time: 10 minutes | Total time: 10 minutes

TURKISH EGGS
WITH YOGHURT

SERVES 2

1 tbsp white wine vinegar

4 large free-range eggs

150g Greek yoghurt

2 garlic cloves, finely grated

2 tbsp butter

1 tsp dried chilli flakes (use Aleppo chilli flakes if you can find them)

1 tsp smoked paprika

1 tbsp extra-virgin olive oil

Small handful of fresh mint leaves, finely chopped

Sea salt and freshly ground black pepper

Toasted sourdough bread, to serve

1 To poach the eggs, fill a wide pan with water to a depth of about 5cm and bring to the boil. Add a pinch of sea salt and the vinegar. Lower the heat to a very gentle simmer and drop the eggs into the water right at the surface (you may find it easier to break each egg into a cup and slide it gently into the water). Cook for 3–4 minutes before removing with a slotted spoon and draining on kitchen paper.

2 Mix together the yoghurt and garlic and set aside.

3 Place a small frying pan over a medium-high heat and add the butter. Allow it to foam and become nutty and golden brown. Turn off the heat and sprinkle in the chilli flakes and paprika. Stir through the oil and set aside.

4 Divide the yoghurt between 2 serving plates, spreading in a circular motion to leave a shallow well. Add 2 poached eggs to each well and sprinkle with chopped fresh mint. Spoon the spiced butter mixture over the top and serve with chunky slices of toasted sourdough.

I have always turned my nose up at stuffed peppers when I see them in books and magazines, deeming them to be a rather retro mishap, akin to the eggs baked in avocado recipes that are doing the rounds on the Internet at the moment. However, after eating a feast of vegetarian food on the Greek island of Ikaria, I have been converted to this simple but highly effective dish. I will note that the stuffed peppers I enjoyed were cooked in a wood-fired oven, washed down with local red wine and a spot of traditional Greek dancing. Perhaps the experience made the dish? Either way, I've been making them at home with great success, even minus the dancing and wine, though that can easily be arranged. You can add potatoes to the baking tin along with the peppers if you'd like a more substantial meal.

Hands-on time: 20 minutes | Total time: 1 hour 20 minutes

STUFFED PEPPERS

SERVES 4

2 tbsp olive oil

1 large onion, finely chopped

3 garlic cloves, crushed

1 tbsp dried oregano

200g white basmati rice

2 x 400g tins chopped tomatoes

500ml vegetable stock

6 large red peppers

Sea salt and freshly ground black pepper

1 Preheat the oven to 200°C (180°C fan).

2 Place a large frying pan over a medium-high heat. Add a drop of olive oil and fry the onion for 6 minutes, until it becomes soft. Stir through the garlic and oregano and fry for another minute or so.

3 Add the rice and tomatoes and cook for 5 minutes, stirring continuously. Pour in the vegetable stock and cook for 10 minutes or so, until the rice is just about cooked, stirring occasionally. Season to taste with salt and pepper and remove from the heat to cool completely.

4 Prepare the peppers by carefully removing the tops and any seeds and core from the inside of each one. Arrange the peppers standing upright in a high-sided baking tin and then fill with the rice mixture. Add about 2 tablespoons of water to each pepper and then brush the edges of the peppers with olive oil.

5 Place the baking tin on the middle shelf of the oven and roast for 40–45 minutes, until the peppers are tender and the rice is fully cooked.

6 Serve with freshly dressed salad leaves for a filling supper.

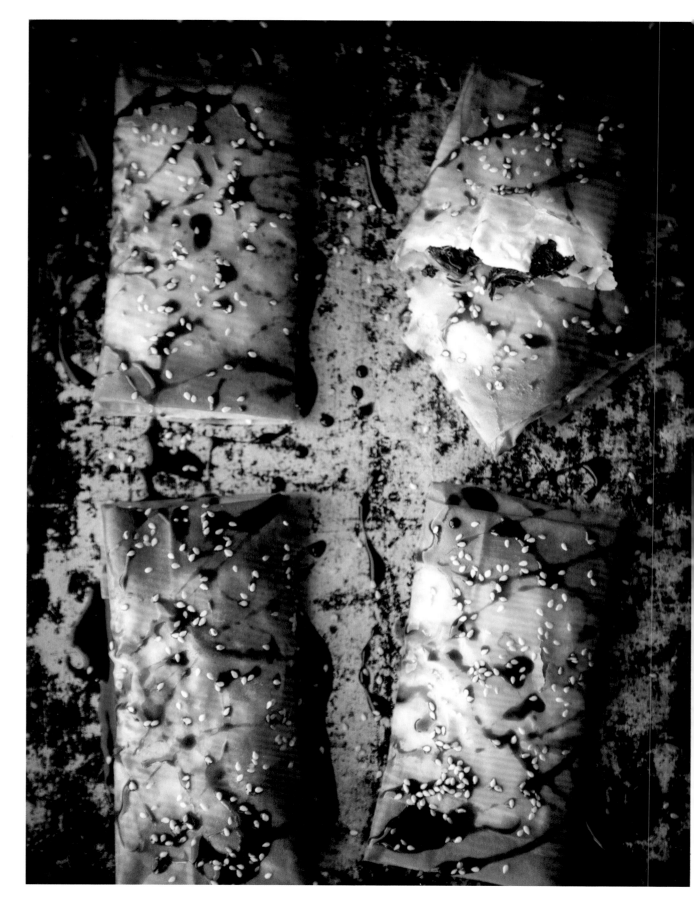

Eleni from Ikaria taught me how to make these wonderfully simple filo pies while we cooked together in her kitchen, high in the mountains on the island of Ikaria. The salty feta, combined with flaky, crisp filo and a drizzle of sweet syrup over the top is truly unique. These pies can be served with a salad as a light supper.

Hands-on time: 30 minutes | **Total time: 50 minutes**

ELENI'S FILO PASTRY PIES

SERVES 4

200g frozen spinach, thawed

Large handful each of fennel fronds, parsley and fresh oregano, roughly chopped

4 sheets of filo pastry, thawed if frozen, each 22 x 26cm

1 large free-range egg, beaten

200g feta cheese, thinly sliced

2 tsp sesame seeds

Sea salt and freshly ground black pepper

Pomegranate molasses, to serve

1 Preheat the oven to 200°C (180°C fan).

2 Using a clean j cloth or kitchen paper squeeze out any excess water from the spinach, then add to a bowl and stir in the chopped herbs. Set aside.

3 Take a sheet of filo pastry (keep the remaining sheets under a damp tea towel to prevent drying out) and brush with beaten egg. Place a quarter of the spinach mixture in the centre of each rectangle. Arrange a couple of slices of feta cheese on top and season with salt and pepper. Fold in both short ends, then fold in the end nearest to you and roll over to form a parcel.

4 Repeat the process until you have four parcels. Place them on a baking sheet and brush the tops with the remaining beaten egg. Sprinkle over sesame seeds and bake in the oven for 20 minutes, until the pastry is crisp and golden.

5 Serve warm from the oven with a drizzle of pomegranate molasses over the top.

There is a street in Bari, a small town on the heel of Italy, where the local ladies sit making orecchiette (small ear-shaped pasta) on makeshift tables, all the while keeping an eye out for potential passing customers. I've been lucky enough to visit twice, and each time I've managed to fail miserably with an audience of expert Italian pasta makers looking on. These ladies have been making orecchiette all their lives – armed only with flour, water and a butter knife they make some of the very best the world has to offer. When you have a simple ingredient it's essential not to overcomplicate things so this is a great way to serve orecchiette, resulting in a silky and salty sauce. At the mercy of the Italian nation, add the zest of 1 lemon for a welcome but not essential sharp bite.

Hands-on time: 30 minutes | Total time: 30 minutes

ORECCHIETTE WITH KALE AND PANGRATTATO

SERVES 4–6

450g Tuscan kale (or similar variety), tough stems trimmed

6 tbsp olive oil

50g coarse sourdough breadcrumbs (at least 1–2 days old is best)

2 large garlic cloves, finely chopped

2 tbsp soft unsalted butter

6 anchovy fillets, drained

½ tsp dried chilli flakes

500g orecchiette

6 tbsp freshly grated Parmesan

Sea salt and freshly ground black pepper

1 Blanch the kale in batches for 3–4 minutes in a large pan of lightly salted water until just tender. Using tongs, transfer to a tray and leave to cool, then squeeze out all the excess water. Chop the leaves and finely chop the stems. Set aside until needed and reserve the cooking water.

2 Heat half of the olive oil in a frying pan over a medium heat. Add the breadcrumbs and cook for about 4 minutes, stirring regularly until they are beginning to brown. Stir in half of the garlic and continue to cook for another 3 minutes, again stirring often until the breadcrumbs are nicely golden. Season with salt and pepper and then transfer to a plate lined with kitchen paper and leave to cool.

3 Heat the butter in a large pan with 2 tablespoons of the remaining oil. Add the anchovies, dried chilli flakes and remaining garlic and cook for 2 minutes, mashing down the anchovies with a wooden spoon to make a paste.

Add the chopped kale and continue to cook for another 3–4 minutes, until the kale is warmed through. Season with salt and pepper to taste.

4 Meanwhile, bring the reserved kale cooking liquid to a rolling boil and cook the pasta according to the packet instructions until al dente. Drain and reserve a cupful of the pasta cooking liquid.

5 Add the pasta along with half a cup of the pasta cooking liquid to the kale and anchovy mixture and stir over a high heat for a couple of minutes, adding a little more of the cooking liquid as needed until the sauce has nicely coated the pasta. Mix in the Parmesan and half of the pangrattato (golden breadcrumbs), tossing to combine.

6 Divide the pasta between bowls and drizzle with the rest of the olive oil, then scatter over the remaining pangrattato to serve.

If ever there was a summer salad to impress, this would be it. Humble though its ingredients are, they are used in such a way as to make the very most of them. Like many bread salads, this one finds its origins in peasant food but makes a hearty dish humming with spice and flavour. Sprinkle with a little extra sumac before serving for a sharp hit of citrus. You could also replace the sourdough with toasted pitta.

Hands-on time: 15 minutes | **Total time: 45 minutes**

MIDDLE EASTERN BREAD SALAD

SERVES 4

5 large mixed peppers

300g sourdough bread, torn into rough bite-sized pieces

Olive oil, for drizzling

500g cherry tomatoes, halved

½ cucumber, peeled, deseeded and diced

½ red onion, thinly sliced

4 radishes, thinly sliced

Large handful of fresh coriander, roughly torn

Large handful of fresh parsley, roughly torn

150g black olives, pitted

FOR THE DRESSING

3 tbsp extra-virgin olive oil

1 tbsp red wine vinegar

Juice of ½ lemon

1 garlic clove, finely grated

1 tsp cumin seeds, toasted

1 tsp sumac

Sea salt and freshly ground black pepper

1 Preheat the oven to 200°C (180°C fan).

2 Place the peppers on a large flat baking tray and bake in the oven for 25 minutes, or until blackened and charred on all sides. Remove the peppers from the tray while still hot, place in a bowl and cover with cling film. The steam in the bowl will allow you to remove the skins easily. When cool enough to handle remove the skins and cores of the peppers and slice into chunky pieces.

3 Place a small handful of the peppers in a food processor with the ingredients for the dressing and blitz until smooth. Season to taste, transfer to a bowl and set aside.

4 Lay the bread pieces out on the same baking tray that you cooked the peppers on, drizzle with a little oil and season with salt and pepper. Place in the oven for 5–6 minutes until just toasted.

5 Place all the remaining salad ingredients in a large mixing bowl and add the peppers, toasted bread and dressing. Toss until completely coated and serve.

This method of cooking chicken thighs is probably one of the best you'll find. You cook them slowly skin side down on a hot griddle pan until the skin becomes sizzling and crisp and only flip them over towards the end to finish cooking through. With an aromatic green marinade they are smoky and sensational served with a crisp salad of crunchy vegetables and herbs.

Hands-on time: 10 minutes | Total time: 40–45 minutes, plus marinating

VIETNAMESE CHICKEN SALAD

SERVES 4

FOR THE CHICKEN

4 large garlic cloves

Thumb-sized piece of fresh ginger, peeled and roughly chopped

1 green chilli, roughly chopped

Zest and juice of 1 lime

Large handful of fresh coriander (leaves and stalks), roughly chopped

1 tbsp fish sauce

8 boneless chicken thighs, skin on

1 tbsp sunflower oil

FOR THE DRESSING

Finely grated zest and juice of 1 lime

3 tbsp fish sauce

2 tbsp caster sugar

1 small Thai red chilli, very finely chopped

FOR THE SALAD

Large handful of fresh mint leaves

Large handful of fresh coriander leaves

200g Chinese cabbage, finely shredded

2 large carrots, cut into fine julienne (on a mandoline is best)

Large handful of salted peanuts, roughly chopped

1 Bash the garlic, ginger, chilli, lime zest and coriander into rough paste, using a pestle and mortar. Mix through the lime juice and fish sauce. Smear the paste all over the chicken thighs. If you have time, cover and leave to marinate overnight, otherwise 30 minutes should do the trick.

2 To cook the chicken, heat a large heavy-based frying pan over a medium heat. Add the sunflower oil to the pan, then place the chicken thighs in it skin side down. Reduce the heat to very low and cook for 20–30 minutes, until the skin is nice and crispy. Don't touch them while they are cooking or shake the pan, just leave them alone and you will produce the most fantastic crisp skin and succulent chicken.

3 When the chicken thighs are nicely browned and the chicken is almost cooked through, turn them over and cook for another 5–6 minutes, until completely cooked through and tender. Transfer to a carving board.

4 Meanwhile, mix all the dressing ingredients together until the sugar has dissolved and put to one side. Put all the ingredients for the salad, except the peanuts, into a large bowl and toss lightly to combine, then add the dressing and toss to coat evenly.

5 To serve, divide the dressed salad between plates and pile the chicken on top. Scatter over the peanuts and serve.

Sweden's mushroom season in the middle of summer is a tense time, when locals guard their picking patches with great secrecy. At this time of the year the forests are teeming with golden trumpet-shaped mushrooms. This recipe makes a simple savoury tart, which can be adapted to use any type of mushrooms or cheese you can get your hands on. While I suggest Västerbottensost, a cheese common in Sweden, you could use a good strong Cheddar or Gruyère. Most good food shops will have a few interesting mushroom varieties on offer so do experiment – this tart is a lovely way to show them off.

Hands-on time: 30 minutes | **Total time: 50 minutes**

SWEDISH CHANTERELLE AND VÄSTERBOTTENSOST TART

SERVES 6

FOR THE PASTRY

225g plain flour

125g chilled butter, diced

3 tbsp cold water

FOR THE FILLING

2 tbsp olive oil

300g chanterelle mushrooms (or any mushrooms you can find)

3 large free-range eggs

200ml double cream

100g Västerbottensost (or use Cheddar or Gruyère), grated

Sea salt and freshly ground black pepper

1 Preheat the oven to 180°C (160°C fan).

2 Tip the flour into a bowl and add the butter. Rub in using your fingertips until the mixture resembles rough breadcrumbs. Add the water and use a round-bladed knife to bring the dough together into a ball. Wrap in cling film and place in the fridge for at least 10 minutes.

3 While the pastry rests, place a large frying pan over a medium heat and add the oil. Fry the mushrooms for 5 minutes, until they are tender and have a nice colour. Remove the pan from the heat and set aside to cool.

4 Roll out the chilled pastry on a lightly floured surface to a thickness of about 5mm and then use it to line a 25cm loose-bottomed fluted tart tin, about 3cm deep. Prick the base with a fork, line with parchment paper and baking beans and bake

in the oven for about 10 minutes. Remove the paper and beans and return to the oven for a further 5 minutes.

5 While the pastry blind bakes, mix together the eggs and cream, whisking to combine. Stir in the cheese and season with salt and pepper.

6 Remove the pastry case from the oven and arrange the cooked mushrooms over the base, then pour in the cheese mixture and bake for about 20 minutes, or until the pie filling is set. Trim the edges of the pastry and allow to cool. Serve in generous slices.

I asked my friend, Hungarian food writer Zsofi Mautner, to share her recipe for a classic Chicken Paprikash with me after a visit to Budapest, but I never could have imagined the complexity of this traditional dish. Clearly well versed in having to explain the differences to confused foreigners, Zsofi, pointed out that Chicken Paprikash is actually a variation of a 'pörkölt', a stew that features less liquid and forgoes the soured cream added at the end. She stresses that the dish is always served with dumplings and is not just a dish saved for tourists, but instead is cooked and eaten as part of everyday life in Hungary.

Hands-on time: 30 minutes | Total time: 2 hours

ZSOFI'S HUNGARIAN CHICKEN PAPRIKASH WITH GALUSKA DUMPLINGS

SERVES 4

75ml sunflower oil

4 large onions, roughly sliced

3 tbsp best-quality Hungarian sweet paprika

8 skin-on chicken thighs

1 green pepper, sliced lengthways

1 tomato

1 tbsp cornflour

200ml soured cream

Sea salt and freshly ground black pepper

FOR THE DUMPLINGS

300g plain flour

Pinch of salt

2 large free-range eggs

1 Heat the oil in a large pan over a medium heat. Add the sliced onions and cook for 6 minutes, until translucent, stirring occasionally. Now comes a secret step: remove the pan from the heat and add the paprika. This is very important – if you add the paprika over the heat, it may burn and acquire a bitter taste. Return to the heat, add the chicken thighs and stir so that the spicy onion mix covers the meat evenly.

2 Pour in about 500ml water, making sure the liquid doesn't completely cover the meat. Add the sliced green pepper, the whole tomato (which will be removed at the end) and season with salt and pepper.

3 Cover and simmer over a very low heat for about 1½ hours. Remove the chicken and whole tomato from the pan and set aside on a plate. Depending on the thickness of the sauce, cook for 10 minutes uncovered, to reduce the liquid slightly.

4 Whisk together the corn flour and soured cream and mix this into the sauce. Slowly bring to a low simmer and cook for 5 minutes until you are left with a spicy, thick sauce. Return the chicken to the pan and toss to coat in the sauce. (You can prepare the dish in advance up to this point – it tastes even better when reheated the following day.)

5 To make the dumplings, tip the flour into a mixing bowl with a pinch of salt and make a well in the centre. Add the eggs and 100ml lukewarm water. Beat together, being careful not to over mix, until a rough dough forms. Using a teaspoon, form into 20 small rough dumplings. Cook these in a large pan of boiling salted water for 4–5 minutes, until tender. Serve with the chicken and toss gently to coat in the sauce.

Ikaria in Greece is one of the five blue zones of the world. These zones have been identified as having the highest concentration of centenarians in the world, where residents are said to live longer, healthier and happier lives than the rest of the world. The Ikarian diet is mainly vegetarian with very little red meat; instead they rely heavily on home-grown fruit and vegetables and local produce. This 'giant bean' stew will instantly transport you to the little Greek island and hopefully add a few years on along the way.

Hands-on time: 15 minutes | Total time: 55 minutes

ELENI'S GIANT BEAN AND TOMATO STEW

SERVES 4

3 onions, very thinly sliced

4 garlic cloves, very thinly sliced

6 tbsp extra-virgin olive oil

2 x 400g tins butter beans, rinsed and drained

3 carrots, thinly sliced

1 x 640g jar passata

2 large beef tomatoes, sliced

Large handful of fresh oregano

Few thyme sprigs

2 bay leaves

300ml vegetable stock

Sea salt and freshly ground black pepper

1 Preheat the oven to 220°C (200°C fan).

2 Place the sliced onions and garlic in a bowl and pour in 4 tablespoons of the olive oil. Season with salt and pepper and then use your hands to massage the onions until they begin to soften down. Set aside.

3 Place the drained butter beans in the base of a large earthenware dish or baking dish. Arrange the carrots on top, pour over the passata and spread out evenly. Scatter the onion mixture across the top, add the tomato slices and press the herbs roughly on top.

4 Pour over the vegetable stock and cover with foil. Place on the middle shelf of the oven and bake for 40 minutes. Serve warm from the oven.

It was deep in an olive grove on Croatia's Istrian coast where I fell in love with this traditional chicken stew. As the sun set, local food lover Goran Zgrablic and his friends taught me to make fuzi, a typical pasta of the region. I would say they were somewhat similar in shape to penne, but Goran laughed off the mere idea, and pointed out their unique differences in shape. Either way the handmade pasta was the ideal accompaniment to zgvacet, a traditional dish of chicken braised with tomatoes, which we savoured with plenty of wine late into the evening.

Hands-on time: 25 minutes | **Total time: 1¼ hours**

CHICKEN ZGVACET

SERVES 4

4 tbsp olive oil

1 whole chicken, cut into portions

2 large onions, finely chopped

2 carrots, finely chopped

1 rosemary sprig

75ml white wine

2 x 400g tins whole plum tomatoes

1 tbsp dried oregano

500ml chicken stock

Sea salt and freshly ground black pepper

250g fresh penne pasta, cooked, to serve

1 Place a large casserole dish over a medium-high heat and add 2 tablespoons of the olive oil. Season the chicken pieces well with salt and pepper and add to the pan in batches. Cook until golden brown on all sides and then transfer to a plate.

2 Add the remaining olive oil to the pan and fry the onion, carrot and rosemary sprig for 6–8 minutes, until the carrot is just tender.

3 Return the chicken to the pan, pour in the wine and allow to bubble for 2 minutes before adding the tomatoes, oregano and chicken stock. Cover with a lid and cook slowly for 1 hour, or until the chicken is completely tender and cooked all the way through. Remove the lid and simmer for a further 15 minutes, until the sauce has thickened slightly. Season to taste

4 Serve the chicken with cooked fresh pasta and a glass of Croatian wine!

It's hard to resist these puddings on the menu at Gjelina in Los Angeles. Subtly sweet toffee pudding topped with tooth-clenching salted caramel and refreshing crème fraîche – delicious. This recipe is perfect for a dinner party as it can all be made ahead of time and popped in the fridge until you're ready to serve. My kind of dessert!

Hands-on time: 25 minutes | Total time: 1½ hours, including chilling

BUTTERSCOTCH PUDDING
WITH SALTED CARAMEL AND CRÈME FRAÎCHE

MAKES 6

4 tbsp soft unsalted butter

150g soft dark brown sugar

225ml single cream

2 tbsp cornflour

½ tsp salt

375ml full-fat milk

3 large egg yolks

1 tsp vanilla extract

250g crème fraîche, to serve

FOR THE SALTED CARAMEL SAUCE

100g butter

150g soft dark brown sugar

3 tbsp golden syrup

150ml double cream

1 tsp vanilla extract

Pinch of sea salt

1 Melt the butter in a medium heavy-based pan. Add the brown sugar and cook for 2–3 minutes, stirring occasionally, until the sugar has dissolved. Add the cream and bring to a simmer, stirring until you have a thick butterscotch sauce.

2 Meanwhile, place the cornflour and salt in a large bowl with a couple of tablespoons of the milk and mix until smooth. Add the rest of the milk and whisk together. Whisk in the egg yolks and vanilla extract and then gradually pour in the hot butterscotch sauce, whisking continuously.

3 Wipe out the pan and then strain the mixture through a fine-mesh sieve back into the pan. Cook over a medium heat for 5–6 minutes, stirring regularly, until the butterscotch custard starts to thicken. Remove from the heat and pour into pretty glasses or ramekins. Chill for at least 1 hour before serving, or up to 3 days.

4 To make the caramel sauce, place the butter, sugar and golden syrup into a pan and bring to a gentle simmer; cook until the sugar has dissolved. Whisk in the cream, vanilla and salt and simmer for 3 minutes until the sauce is thick and sticky. Use straight away or transfer to a jar, leave to cool and chill until needed – the sauce will keep for up to 7 days in the fridge.

5 To serve, drizzle the puddings with caramel sauce, top with a dollop of crème fraîche and add a final drizzle of sauce.

An elegant variation of Sweden's ris à la malta, a creamy rice pudding. This version features that irresistible element of a crème brûlée, the caramelised sugar topping. A real treat and a great dinner party dessert.

Hands-on time: 20 minutes | Total time: 45–55 minutes, plus chilling

RICE PUDDING WITH CARAMEL TOPPING

SERVES 4

100g pearl or pudding rice

Pinch of salt

2 tsp butter

750ml full-fat milk

1 vanilla pod, split lengthways and seeds scraped

Finely grated zest of 1 orange

1 tbsp honey

4 tbsp dark brown sugar

1 Add the rice, salt and butter to a large pan with 200ml water, then cover with a lid and place over a high heat. Bring to the boil then reduce the heat and simmer for 8–10 minutes, or until the water has been absorbed and the rice is cooked.

2 Pour in the milk, vanilla pod and seeds, orange zest and honey. Stir through to combine, cover, then bring to the boil again. Reduce the heat and simmer slowly for 25–30 minutes, until you have a creamy consistency but the rice still has a little bite to it.

3 Pour the rice pudding into 4 individual ramekins and allow to cool before covering and popping it in the fridge until chilled.

4 When ready to serve sprinkle the tops with sugar and use a kitchen blowtorch to caramelise the sugar. (Alternatively you can place the ramekins under a very hot grill for a few seconds, just until the sugar melts.)

STREET EATS

———

Thai Breakfast Omelette

———

Crispy Fried Chinese Eggs

———

Lahmacun

———

Portuguese Gazpacho with Grilled Sardines

———

Tuna and Tomato Mozzarella Salad

———

Maria's Polenta Chips

———

Asian Beef Noodle Salad

———

Korean Fried Chicken

———

Vietnamese Beef Noodle Stir Fry

———

Polish Blueberry Pierogi

———

Chocolate Hazelnut Cigars

———

I think it's my inner cheapskate that obsesses over just how inexpensive street food can be, while the food lover in me swoons over the expertly prepared dishes alive with flavour. It never ceases to amaze me how some of the best food I've tried around the world tends to cost next to nothing. I'm always wowed by stalls that make the same dish day in day out, slowly perfecting them over years with the same key ingredients and limited equipment.

Hanoi in Vietnam has to be the street food capital of the world. Nowhere else have I been where there are so many different amazing dishes served from roadside vendors. Barbecued meat in rich broths with noodles and fresh herbs; crispy sweet potato and prawn cakes; and spicy beef and shredded papaya salad – all made to order in a matter of mouth-watering moments. I get ultimate satisfaction attempting to recreate these wonderful dishes at home. Of course, they never taste quite as good back home but they bring back great memories, and isn't that what food should be all about?

These recipes are just some favourites from my recent travels and are easy to make at home. A Vietnamese beef noodle stir fry which is my take on the street food classic bun cha, iced gazpacho with grilled sardine toasts from my visit to Lisbon and a Thai breakfast omelette inspired by an early start at a floating market in Bangkok – all these instantly bring back fantastic memories of wonderful travels and great street food enjoyed along the way.

When I was on my travels one of the best breakfasts I had was this Thai omelette. It's quick to make – with just a few simple ingredients you have a fresh and healthy breakfast in a matter of minutes!

Hands-on time: 8 minutes | Total time: 8 minutes

THAI BREAKFAST OMELETTE

SERVES 1

1 tbsp sunflower oil

2 large free-range eggs

Handful of beansprouts, plus a few to garnish

2 spring onions, thinly sliced

Generous handful of chopped fresh coriander, plus extra to garnish

½ red chilli, thinly sliced

Small handful of salted peanuts, crushed, plus extra to garnish

1 tbsp fish sauce

Juice of ½ lime

1 tsp caster sugar

1 Add the sunflower oil to a wok and place over a high heat. While it is heating up (you need it nice and hot), loosely whisk the eggs in a bowl.

2 Once the wok is smoking hot, pour the beaten egg into the base and move it around so that it coats the sides and bottom completely. It will cook very quickly. Add the beansprouts, spring onions, coriander, chilli and crushed peanuts.

3 When you notice the edges of the egg becoming golden brown, fold back the cooked egg to create a parcel over the other ingredients. Press it down to make sure everything is nice and compact and slide onto a serving plate.

4 Meanwhile combine the fish sauce, lime juice and caster sugar in a jar with a tight-fitting lid and shake well to combine – a few flecks of chopped red chilli is nice here too if you fancy a bit of a kick in the morning!

5 Garnish the omelette parcel with beansprouts, chopped coriander and a final scattering of peanuts and serve with the dressing.

These crispy fried eggs, inspired by Australian food writer and chef Kylie Kwong, are a satisfying solution to the never-ending dilemma of 'what's for dinner'. While they might not be a feast, they are certainly a rewarding and simple supper, requiring only a handful of ingredients, which, more often than not, I have to hand. If you happen to have some leftover boiled rice that you can serve with the eggs, you are in business. Otherwise indulge in them just as they are –spicy, crunchy and gloriously gooey.

Hands-on time: 5 minutes | Total time: 5 minutes

CRISPY FRIED CHINESE EGGS

SERVES 1

3 tbsp rapeseed oil

2 large free-range eggs

2 tbsp oyster sauce, plus extra for drizzling

1 red chilli, thinly sliced

2–3 spring onions, thinly sliced

1 tbsp sesame seeds, toasted

1 Heat the oil in a wok over a high heat until just before it begins to smoke.

2 Break in the eggs and fry for 2–3 minutes, until they become crisp and golden. Drizzle over the oyster sauce and sprinkle with chilli and spring onions just before the end of the cooking time.

3 Remove from the pan and serve up with an extra drizzle of oyster sauce and a sprinkle of sesame seeds.

One thing you begin to notice when you travel and eat street food regularly is just how expertly the vendors have mastered their craft. Years of repeating the same dish and actions over and over might seem tiresome, but of the many I've met there is huge pride attached to the process. This proved to be true when I met the owner of Öz Kilis Kebap Salonu, a restaurant in Istanbul famous for its lahmacun. He had been making these crispy meat flatbreads in exactly the same way since he was a young boy and they are truly delicious. It is essential you cook these in a screaming hot oven and that you make sure you roll the dough out as thinly as you can.

Hands-on time: 30 minutes | Total time: 1½–2 hours

LAHMACUN

SERVES 4

FOR THE DOUGH

300g strong white flour or '00' flour, plus extra for dusting

1 tsp salt

175ml tepid water

1 tsp caster sugar

7g sachet fast action dried yeast

1 tbsp olive oil

FOR THE TOPPING

1 red pepper, roughly chopped

1 green pepper, roughly chopped

1 onion, roughly chopped

350g lamb mince

Large handful of flat-leaf parsley, roughly chopped, plus extra to serve

2 tsp ground coriander

2 tsp ground cumin

1 tsp red chilli flakes

Salt

TO SERVE

¼ head iceberg lettuce, finely shredded

2 large tomatoes, sliced

Juice of ½ lemon

1 In a large mixing bowl combine the flour and salt and make a well in the centre. Mix the tepid water with the sugar, yeast and olive oil in a jug and whisk until combined. Pour this mixture into the well and using a wooden spoon or your hands mix together to form a rough dough.

2 Turn the dough out on a floured work surface and knead for 10 minutes, or until the dough becomes smooth and elastic. Place back in the bowl and cover with cling film. Leave the dough in a warm place to rise for 50 minutes, or until it has doubled in size.

3 Meanwhile prepare the topping. Place the peppers and onion in a food processor and blitz until finely chopped. Transfer to a clean kitchen towel, wrap into a tight ball and squeeze over a sink to get rid of as much liquid as you can. Skipping this step will mean the topping will be too wet for the dough. Place the vegetables in a large bowl with the lamb mince, parsley, coriander, cumin and chilli flakes. Season generously with salt and mix thoroughly to combine.

4 Place a pizza stone or large flat baking tray in the oven and preheat to 225°C (210°C fan).

5 Punch down the risen dough with your knuckles and then divide it into 4 small balls or 2 large ones, depending how big you want your bases to be. Sprinkle your work surface with a little flour and roll out each ball into as thin a circle as possible. Using a fork, spread the minced meat mixture in a thin layer over the top, making sure you spread it right to the edges. Cook one flatbread at a time on the pizza stone for 10 minutes, or until the dough is crisp.

6 Serve the flatbreads straight from the oven. Add a small handful of lettuce, some sliced tomato, a squeeze of lemon juice and a little parsley and roll up.

Lisbon's Time Out Mercado Da Ribeira is a haven for food lovers. Originally built in 1892, the market has recently been refurbished with 35 kiosks hosting some of the cities finest food offerings. I met local chef Alexandre Silva there and he taught me to make this Portuguese classic, which he serves with a grilled sardine sandwich. An instant summer treat!

Hands-on time: 20 minutes | **Total time: 25 minutes**

PORTUGUESE GAZPACHO
WITH GRILLED SARDINES

SERVES 4

4 slices of sourdough toast

1 garlic clove

2 tbsp olive oil

8 small fresh sardines

Sea salt

FOR THE GAZPACHO

1 small onion, roughly chopped

4 large fresh tomatoes, roughly chopped

1 small cucumber, peeled, deseeded and roughly chopped

1 slice of sourdough bread

75ml extra-virgin olive oil, plus extra for drizzling

1 tbsp white wine vinegar

1 tsp dried oregano

Large handful of ice cubes

Sea salt and freshly ground black pepper

1 Place all the ingredients for the gazpacho in a high-speed blender along with 50ml cold water and blitz until completely smooth. Season to taste with salt and pepper and then chill until you are ready to serve.

2 Rub each slice of sourdough toast with the cut side of the garlic clove and drizzle with olive oil. Lay the sardines on the toast and place under a moderate grill for 4–5 minutes, until the skin is just crisp. Drizzle with a little more olive oil and sprinkle with sea salt.

3 Pour the gazpacho into serving glasses and drizzle with a little extra olive oil. Serve the sardine toasts with the gazpacho on the side.

Polignano a Mare is a true slice of Italian seaside life! The birthplace of one of Italy's most famous singers, Domenico Modugno, and home to one of the countries most beautiful coastlines, this small town has some great places to eat. When I visited Pescaria, a fairly new restaurant run by chef Lucio Mele, was making a name for itself for its new take on Italian street food inspired by the sea. Crispy fried octopus was paired with ricotta, drizzled with a red wine reduction and sandwiched between a crispy tortoiseshell bread bap, challenging the classic Italian rule of not combining cheese and fish. I've done something similar here, although you should really only use the best ingredients you can get your hands on for this one.

Hands-on time: 10 minutes | **Total time: 10 minutes**

TUNA AND TOMATO MOZZARELLA SALAD

SERVES 4

75g rocket

100g baby salad leaves

350g sushi-grade tuna, cubed

350g cherry tomatoes, halved

½ red onion, very thinly sliced

2 tbsp capers

2 large balls buffalo mozzarella, roughly cubed

50g pistachio nuts

Extra-virgin olive oil

Squeeze of lemon juice

Sea salt and freshly ground black pepper

1 Arrange the rocket and salad leaves over the base of a large serving platter. Scatter over the remaining ingredients, except the oil and lemon juice, making sure they are evenly distributed.

2 Drizzle generously with olive oil and squeeze over some lemon juice. Season sparingly with salt and pepper. Toss gently and then serve with an extra glug of olive oil.

Easily one the most bizarre cooking sequences I have ever filmed for TV was shot on the hot streets of Bari with 90-year-old local legend Maria. She stopped us as we were about to leave, disgusted that we hadn't bothered to film her! The whole crew was dragged over to her stoop as she fired up a cauldron filled with oil, practically the size of her, to cook us these sgagliozze, or polenta chips. I was dripping in sweat from the late summer heat as she continued to scold me in Italian for not cooking them correctly – a trait I've since learned is quite common among Italians of a certain generation! After a lot of laughing she sent us packing with a steaming hot brown paper bag of sgagliozze sprinkled with salt, having fleeced us for whatever money we had. A real hustler and a true character!

Hands-on time: 20 minutes | Total time: 20 minutes, plus setting

MARIA'S POLENTA CHIPS

SERVES 4

1 litre chicken stock

1 x 250g packet instant polenta

Sunflower oil, for frying

Sea salt

1 Grease a 22 x 30cm baking tin with oil and set aside.

2 Bring the chicken stock to the boil in a large pan. Using a whisk, gradually add the polenta, whisking until it is all incorporated. Cook gently for about 2 minutes until the polenta is soft or according the packet instructions.

3 Pour the polenta into the prepared tin, allow to cool and cover. Chill in the fridge to set for 3–4 hours or overnight. Once set, remove from the tin and cut into 5 x 10cm slices.

4 Pour the sunflower oil into a high-sided non-stick pan to a depth of about 5cm and place over a medium-high heat. When the oil reaches a temperature of 180°C (use a kitchen thermometer or drop in a small cube of polenta and wait until it sizzles), fry the polenta chips in batches for about 5 minutes, or until they are golden brown, turning occasionally. Transfer to a plate lined with kitchen paper and sprinkle generously with sea salt. For true authenticity, serve hot in a brown paper bag a la Maria!

This is a variation on the classic Thai dish, Beef Laab, a spicy minced beef salad from the northeast of Thailand, usually served with steamed sticky rice. Here I've used the spicy beef mixture as the main element of a fresh-tasting noodle salad. This dish can be topped with toasted sesame seeds, chopped toasted peanuts or ground toasted sticky rice.

Hands-on time: 25 minutes | Total time: 35 minutes

ASIAN BEEF NOODLE SALAD

SERVES 4

FOR THE SPICY BEEF

1 tbsp sunflower oil

250g beef mince

2 garlic cloves, finely chopped

1 red chilli, deseeded and finely chopped

Thumb-sized piece of fresh ginger, peeled and finely chopped

6 spring onions, thinly sliced

1 tbsp dark soy sauce

3 tbsp fish sauce

Juice of 1 lime

1 tsp sesame oil

1 tbsp brown sugar

Small handful of fresh basil

Small handful of fresh coriander

1–2 tbsp toasted sesame seeds, to garnish

FOR THE SALAD

250g rice noodles

3 large bok choy, finely shredded

1 ripe mango, peeled and diced

2 carrots, cut into thin julienne

1 Soak the rice noodles for 5–10 minutes in a large bowl of boiling water, or according to the packet instructions. When the noodles are tender, drain and rinse under cold water. Set aside.

2 Heat the sunflower oil in a large frying pan over a medium-high heat. Fry the beef mince for 5–6 minutes, breaking it up with a wooden spatula, until just browned and any liquid has evaporated. Stir through the garlic, chilli, ginger and half the spring onions. Fry for a further 2 minutes until aromatic.

3 Mix together the soy sauce, fish sauce, lime juice, sesame oil and brown sugar. Add this mixture to the beef and stir through for another 3 minutes, until the liquid has evaporated slightly. Remove from the heat and tear in the basil and coriander. Stir through until combined.

4 To serve, place a pile of rice noodles in the centre of each plate. Add the shredded bok choy, mango chunks and shredded carrot around the sides and then pile a generous spoonful of the minced beef mix on top. Sprinkle with toasted sesame seeds and the remaining sliced spring onions. Eat straight away, while the beef is still warm.

Unfortunately never having been to Korea, I've had to make do and try these addictive chicken wings in London. I can report that this fried chicken really means business! Lightly battered crispy chicken in a sweet and spicy Korean chilli paste sauce is completely and utterly addictive.

Hands-on time: 30 minutes | Total time: 30 minutes

KOREAN FRIED CHICKEN

SERVES 4

Sunflower oil, for frying

125g flour

1 tbsp cornflour

½ tsp baking powder

Generous pinch of salt

16 chicken wings

1 tbsp toasted sesame seeds

FOR THE SAUCE

8 garlic cloves, finely grated

Large thumb-sized piece of fresh ginger, peeled and finely grated

6 tbsp light soy sauce

10 tbsp gochujang (Korean chilli paste)

4 tbsp rice vinegar

2 tbsp sesame oil

6 tbsp dark brown sugar

1 In a small pan whisk together all the ingredients for the sauce. Place the pan over a medium heat and bring to a low simmer, cooking until the sugar is just dissolved (this should take about 3 minutes). Set aside while you cook the chicken.

2 Fill a medium pan with sunflower oil until it reaches a depth of about 6cm. Place over a medium heat and heat to 180°C. If you don't have a kitchen thermometer you can test the temperature by dropping in a cube of bread – it should sizzle and turn golden in about 20 seconds.

3 Meanwhile whisk together the flour, cornflour, baking powder and salt with 125ml cold water until you have a smooth, runny batter. Coat the chicken wings in this batter.

4 Working in two batches, carefully add the chicken wings to the oil one at a time, shaking off any excess batter as you go. Fry for 8 minutes until the wings are golden brown and cooked all the way through. Drain using a slotted spoon and place on a plate lined with kitchen paper.

5 When all the chicken is cooked, toss in the warm hot sauce until completely coated. Serve the wings sprinkled with sesame seeds.

The food of South East Asia and in particular Vietnam continues to excite me. The streets of the capital city Hanoi, are lined with food vendors, each one specialising in their trademark street food snack. For very little money you can experience a dish that has been mastered by repetition and championed by local diners who vote on their favourite dish with their feet. While it may seem like this dish has a lot of ingredients, this simple beef noodle dish can be made in a few minutes and should evoke the taste and smell of Vietnam's busiest street food alleys.

Hands-on time: 15 minutes | Total time: 35 minutes

VIETNAMESE BEEF NOODLE STIR FRY

SERVES 4

600g rump steak, trimmed of fat and thinly sliced

3 tbsp fish sauce

2 garlic cloves, very finely chopped

1 lemongrass stalk, roughly bashed and finely sliced

1 tbsp rapeseed oil

4 shallots or 1 large onion, thinly sliced

Roasted peanuts, roughly chopped, to serve

FOR THE SALAD

250g flat rice noodles, cooked and cooled

Large handful of beansprouts

1 cucumber, halved and sliced thinly

Large handful of fresh mint leaves, roughly chopped, plus extra to garnish

Large handful of fresh coriander leaves, roughly chopped

FOR THE NUOC CHAM DRESSING

4 tbsp fish sauce

Juice of 1 lime

1 tbsp caster sugar

1 garlic clove, finely chopped

3 red and green chillies, finely chopped

1 Place the beef strips in a bowl and add the fish sauce, half the garlic and half the lemongrass. Leave to marinate for 20 minutes while you prepare the remaining ingredients.

2 Whisk together all the ingredients for the dressing until the sugar has dissolved, then loosen with 2 tablespoons of water. Set aside.

3 Divide the cooked and cooled noodles between 4 deep bowls and top with the beansprouts, cucumber and herbs.

4 Heat a wok or frying pan over a high heat. Add the oil and just as it begins to smoke add the remaining garlic and lemongrass and shallots to the wok. Stir-fry for 1–2 minutes, until it becomes aromatic. Immediately add the beef and the marinade and stir-fry for 2–3 minutes, allowing it to sit in the pan every now and then without stirring to ensure it gets a good colour and chars slightly.

5 Divide the contents of the pan between the 4 bowls and top with the roasted peanuts. Spoon over the dressing and garnish with a few mint leaves. Serve while the beef is still warm.

Despite Ireland's massive Polish population I had managed to miss out on a taste of their traditional pierogi until quite recently. That all changed when I visited Krakow and got to try these soft poached dumplings filled with a wide variety of savoury fillings – and these sweet ones too. I got roped into a pierogi masterclass from a local expert and I have to admit they are totally delicious and make a lovely dessert.

Hands-on time: 30 minutes | **Total time: 1½ hours**

POLISH BLUEBERRY PIEROGI

SERVES 6

350g plain flour, plus extra for dusting

2 tbsp icing sugar

1 large free-range egg

150ml tepid water

225g frozen blueberries, thawed slightly

FOR THE BLUEBERRY SOURED CREAM

250g soured cream

25g icing sugar, sifted

1 tsp vanilla bean paste

Fresh blueberries

1 Sift the flour and icing sugar into a large bowl and mix to combine. Make a well in the centre and add the egg and tepid water. Using a wooden spoon, work the liquid into the dry ingredients until you have a rough dough.

2 Turn the dough out onto a lightly floured surface and knead for 5 minutes or until it becomes slightly elastic in texture. Shape into a ball, cover with cling film and place in the fridge to rest for 30 minutes. Meanwhile, mix together all the ingredients for the blueberry soured cream in a small bowl and set aside.

3 Divide the dough into two and roll out the first half on a lightly floured surface to a thickness of about 3mm. Using a pastry cutter or a glass, cut out 10cm rounds – you should get 12 rounds. Place a heaped teaspoon of blueberries on each circle, slightly off-centre, and then fold the dough over the berries to form a semicircle. Pinch the edges to seal. Repeat with the remaining dough and blueberries.

4 Bring a large pan of water to the boil and cook the dumplings in batches for 3 minutes, or until they start floating to the surface. Drain with a slotted spoon, shaking off any excess water. Serve the pierogi warm with a generous dollop of the sweetened sour cream and some fresh blueberries scattered over the top.

Completely indulgent and surprisingly easy to make, these filo pastry chocolate cigars make for an altogether different dessert. They are inspired by a visit to a baklava factory in Istanbul, where the bakers worked in a cloud of cornflour, rolling out paper-thin sheets of filo pastry and transforming them into mouthwatering pistachio-filled treats. Bakers can train for years just to learn how to roll out the dough or cut the baklava but don't worry – this incredible intricacy won't be required for these cigars!

Hands-on time: 50 minutes | Total time: 1 hour

CHOCOLATE HAZELNUT CIGARS

MAKES 16

100g toasted skinned hazelnuts, finely chopped, plus extra to decorate

100g dark chocolate, finely chopped or grated (70% cocoa solids)

50g caster sugar

1 tsp honey

4 sheets of filo pastry, thawed if frozen

60g unsalted butter, melted

FOR THE WHITE CHOCOLATE DIP

40g unsalted butter

100g white chocolate, finely chopped

50ml single cream

Icing sugar, to dust

1 Preheat the oven to 180°C (160°C fan) and line a baking tray with parchment paper. In a small bowl, mix together the hazelnuts, dark chocolate, caster sugar and honey.

2 Take one sheet of filo pastry and brush it with melted butter, keeping the remainder covered with a damp tea towel to prevent it from drying out. Cut the pastry widthways into four equal strips. Put a tablespoon of the chocolate-nut mixture at the top of each strip, then roll them up into cigar shapes. Repeat with the remaining pastry sheets and chocolate-nut mixture.

3 Arrange the cigars on the baking sheet and bake for 12–15 minutes, or until crisp and golden.

4 Meanwhile make the white chocolate dip. Melt the butter and white chocolate in a heatproof bowl set over a pan of simmering water (making sure the base of the bowl doesn't touch the water), stirring occasionally. Remove from the heat and fold in the cream and then allow to cool. This can be served chilled or at room temperature – whichever you prefer.

5 Arrange the chocolate hazelnut filo cigars on a platter or individual plates and dust with icing sugar and scatter over the extra chopped hazelnuts to decorate. Serve with a bowl of the white chocolate dip.

INDEX

ACKNOWLEDGEMENTS

Putting the finishing touches to a cookbook always comes with a huge sense of relief and elation. Each one is it's own little mountain that needs climbing and there is always such a great deal of work which goes into it. As much I'd like to take all the credit, there was a brilliant team helping me to create Eat. Live. Go. A huge thank you for your patience, a giant high five and a big old squeeze goes to:

Sarah Hammond, the most patient and delightful editor I have ever come across, thank you for steering the ship so effortlessly.

Rosemary Scoular, for your constant guiding light and for bringing your classic sense of decorum and bloody good fun to proceedings.

Vero and Caitriona, the Hodder PR machine dream team, who make publicity and marketing an absolute dream.

Louise Leffler, for not buckling under the weight of the giant archive of images we threw at you and instead creating another beautifully designed cookbook.

Clare Sayer, for editing up a storm and making sense of my manuscript.

Lizzie Kamenetkzy, for your spectacular food styling. You are honestly one of the best – no one breaks an egg as stylishly. And, of course, the dream team you are flanked by, Poppy, Charlotte, and Katie, who put up with my eighties power ballad playlists in the studio.

Olivia Wardle, for ducking and diving through the under appreciated minefield that is prop styling and pulling together beautiful set-ups.

Sarah Watchorn, for your brilliant and patient recipe testing.

My travel buddies and pals and production teams at Appetite, Nomos, InProduction, Grandma's Boy, Athena and all at RTE, FOX and Food Network for some epic adventures over the last few years.

The brilliant characters and guides I've met on my travels who have shared their knowledge and recipes.

My parents Liz and Dermot, who have been a source of constant support throughout the writing of this book; looking after Max while Sofie and I ping pong back and forth between continents and for always looking out for us.

Joanna Carley, for keeping an element of calm in the madness of what we do and for generally being brilliant and keeping the ship afloat.

Lastly to Sofie for her patience, kindness and generosity. Thank you for putting up with the madness and helping me dream bigger dreams – I couldn't do it without you.

Find me at donalskehan.com and on YouTube, Instagram, Facebook, Twitter, Pinterest, and SnapChat: DonalSkehan.

First published in Great Britain in 2016 by Hodder & Stoughton
An Hachette UK company

1

Recipes and photography copyright © Donal Skehan 2016
Additional photography copyright © Sofie Skehan 2016

The right of Donal Skehan to be identified as the Author of the Work has been asserted by him in accordance with the Copyright, Designs and Patents Act 1988.

All rights reserved. No part of this publication may be reproduced, stored in a retrieval system, or transmitted, in any form or by any means without the prior written permission of the publisher, nor be otherwise circulated in any form of binding or cover other than that in which it is published and without a similar condition being imposed on the subsequent purchaser.

A CIP catalogue record for this title is available from the British Library

Hardback ISBN 978 1 473 64011 5
Ebook ISBN 978 1 473 64010 8

Commissioning Editor: Sarah Hammond
Copy Editor: Clare Sayer
Designer: Louise Leffler
Photographer: Donal Skehan
Food Stylist: Lizzie Kamenetkzy
Props Stylist: Olivia Wardle

Typeset in Giacomo
Printed and bound by Firmengruppe, APPL.

Hodder & Stoughton policy is to use papers that are natural, renewable and recyclable products and made from wood grown in sustainable forests. The logging and manufacturing processes are expected to conform to the environmental regulations of the country of origin.

Hodder & Stoughton Ltd
Carmelite House, 50 Victoria Embankment
London EC4Y 0DZ
www.hodder.co.uk

Marine Branch
Brainse Marglann Mhuirine
Tel: 8336297

Leabharlanna Poiblí Chathair Bhaile Átha Cliath
Dublin City Public Libraries